Promise and Prayer

Promise and Prayer

The Biblical Writings in the Light of Speech-Act Theory

ANTHONY C. THISELTON

CASCADE *Books* • Eugene, Oregon

PROMISE AND PRAYER
The Biblical Writings in the Light of Speech Act Theory

Copyright © 2020 Anthony C. Thiselton. All rights reserved. Except for brief quotations in critical publications or reviews, no part of this book may be reproduced in any manner without prior written permission from the publisher. Write: Permissions, Wipf and Stock Publishers, 199 W. 8th Ave., Suite 3, Eugene, OR 97401.

Cascade Books
An Imprint of Wipf and Stock Publishers
199 W. 8th Ave., Suite 3
Eugene, OR 97401

www.wipfandstock.com

PAPERBACK ISBN: 978-1-7252-5360-5
HARDCOVER ISBN: 978-1-7252-5361-2
EBOOK ISBN: 978-1-7252-5362-9

Cataloging-in-Publication data:

Names: Thiselton, Anthony C., author.

Title: Promise and prayer : the biblical writings in the light of speech act theory / Anthony C. Thiselton.

Description: Eugene, OR : Cascade Books, 2020 | Includes bibliographical references and index.

Identifiers: ISBN 978-1-7252-5360-5 (paperback) | ISBN 978-1-7252-5361-2 (hardcover) | ISBN 978-1-7252-5362-9 (ebook)

Subjects: LCSH: Speech acts (Linguistics). | Language and languages—Religious aspects—Christianity. | Word of God (Christian theology). | Prayer. | Covenants—Biblical teaching.

Classification: LCC BT180 T44 2020 (print) | LCC BT180 (ebook)

OCTOBER 26, 2020

Contents

Acknowledgments | vii

Introduction: Promise and Prayer as Interpersonal Acts of God | 1

Part I: Promise in the Biblical Writings
1 Promise as a Speech Act | 9
2 Promises of God in the Old Testament | 21
3 God's Promises in the New Testament | 31
4 Do All Biblical Promises Apply Universally? | 37

Part II: Prayer in the Biblical Writings
5 The Range of Types of Prayer in the Bible | 43
6 Can Some Prayers Be Said to Constitute Speech Acts? | 52
7 Prayers of Blessing: Are These "Weaker" Speech Acts? | 55
8 Praise and Thanksgiving as Speech Acts | 61
9 Requests: Prayers That Led to Changes in Situations | 68

Concluding Summary | 76

Appendix: Developments in Speech-Act Theory and Biblical Studies | 81

Bibliography | 103
Index of Biblical References | 109
Index of Names | 113
Index of Subjects | 115

Acknowledgments

THERE IS NO NEED for a Preface because I have stressed the pivotal importance of promise and prayer in the summary, conclusion, and throughout. Nevertheless I should like to record my gratitude to Rev, Dr. Robin Parry of Wipf and Stock for wise advice in the shaping and sequence of this book.

Introduction

Promise and Prayer as Interpersonal Acts of God

BOTH THE PROMISES OF God and prayers to God inspired by the Holy Spirit are deeply inter-personal. They entail personal address and encounter. Further, the promises of God disclose what Pannenberg calls "the temporal (or time-related) structure of faith and therefore its nature as trust (corresponding to God's Word of promise)" as especially emphasized by Martin Luther.[1] Pannenberg adds, "The promises put the human present, with the pain of its incompleteness and failure, in the light of God. . . . The concept of promise links our present to God's future."[2] God's faithfulness to his promise becomes apparent not instantly but over a duration of time. It concerns time and history.

Prayer includes many modes of humankind's communicative relation with God. It instantiates what Martin Buber, the Jewish theologian, called an "I-Thou" relationship with God, in which both God and humans are fully and utterly personal. Buber writes, "There is no 'I' as such, but only the word-pair I-You."[3] The I-You relation characterizes God-in-relation-to-humans, and human beings in relation to God. The relation of God and humans to ordinary objects or things in the world is better expressed as

---

1. Pannenberg, *Systematic Theology*, vol. 3, 138.
2. Pannenberg, *Systematic Theology*, vol. 3, 545.
3. Buber, *I and Thou*, 54.

Promise and Prayer

"I-it." Promises are also addressed directly to "you," and usually not through some third person.

At its highest, prayer is best seen as *a "divine dialogue."* Prayer is prompted by the Holy Spirit, addressed to God the Father, and mediated through Jesus Christ, at least in the Christian tradition.[4] Paul writes, "You did not receive a Spirit of slavery to fall back into fear, but you have received a Spirit of adoption. When we cry, 'Abba! Father!' it is that very Spirit bearing witness with our spirit that we are children of God" (Rom 8:15-16). He continues, "The Spirit helps us in our weakness; for we do not know how to pray as we ought, but that very Spirit intercedes with sighs too deep for words. And God, who searches the heart, knows what is in the mind of the Spirit, because the Spirit intercedes for the saints according to the will of God" (Rom 8:26-27). Such theology is expounded further in a Church of England Doctrine Report, duly supported and signed by all sixteen members of the Commission.[5]

This strikes exactly the correct keynote for approaching prayer in the Christian and biblical tradition and in this book. Prayer is not initiated by human beings and passed on to God, as if awaiting an "answer." Prayer is *prompted by God*, and *channeled through human beings*, then to *return again to God*. In this respect, both prayer and promise can be understood as acts of God, mediated and appropriated by humankind. Promise (especially the promises of God) and prayer are essential to our personal communion with God. Prayer and God's promises are both initiated by God in deeply inter-personal relationships.

The promises of God also constitute pledges, guarantees, and commitments. They bind God to act in given ways. Through promise God chooses to limit his freedom by acting only in accordance with what he has promised. The promises of God are also intimately related to *his covenants* with humankind. One of the main arguments of this book is that normally they constitute speech acts, which function in a distinctive way in contrast to

---

4. Church of England Doctrine Commission, "God as Trinity: An Approach through Prayer," 108; cf. 104-21.

5. Church of England Doctrine Commission, *We Believe in God* (1987).

Introduction

propositions or statements. On the other hand, they often presuppose or imply propositions. We shall explicate this claim in our first main chapter.

In the context of modern speech-act theory God's *covenant* may be described as "an institutional fact." As we shall see, these are different from "brute facts." The promissory nature of baptism and the Lord's Supper has been emphasized by Calvin and many others. The Christian sacraments as entailing God's promise also constitute institutional facts.

God's promise, especially as a speech act, changes situations in the world and history. Because God's promise is his sovereign commitment, this claim is relatively uncontroversial. Whether some forms of prayer change reality may be more debatable, but we shall argue that in some or many cases petitionary prayer is capable of changing situation in the world, if it is truly inspired by the Spirit of God. This is one reason why our introductory comments remain crucial to our argument. When we come to examine speech-act theory more closely, we shall note that, as Steven Davis emphasizes, this linguistic theory is "anti-individualist"; it presupposes a duality of one who speaks and one who listens.[6]

Since speech-act theory plays a part in our main argument, we may note that in broad outline it is not an exclusively modern concept. If it is shorn of its modern technicalities, William Tyndale (1494–1536) first stressed that the biblical writings do not merely inform or communicate ideas; they *perform acts*. They convey the promises of God. The Bible, Tyndale explained, "maketh a man's heart glad"; it proclaims "joyful tidings"; it "nameth to be heirs"; it "appoints," "gives," "condemns," "blesses," and so on.[7] Tyndale lists eighteen actions that we may loosely call speech acts. This is not to deny that speech-act theory advanced hugely in the modern era with the insights of J. L. Austin, John Searle, François Recanati, Donald Evans, and many others. But Tyndale pioneered the instinct to regard God's speaking as his act, especially in promise.

---

6. Davis, "Anti-Individualism and Speech-Act Theory."
7. Tyndale, *A Pathway into the Holy Scriptures*, 7–29.

Speech acts, we shall see, are more than simply acts, but not less. Speech acts perform acts *in* the very speaking of them. Austin distinguishes performative "illocutions," as he calls them, which operate with institutional force, from "perlocutions," which have causal force. He writes, "The illocutionary act . . . has a certain *force* in saying something; the perlocutionary act . . . is *the achieving* of certain *effects* by saying something."[8] In biblical studies rhetoric operates with perlocutionary or causal force. When Barth, Bultmann, and Ebeling expound God's word as "event," they come near, but only near, to what Austin, Searle, Evans, and Recanati mean by illocutions or speech acts.

Donald Evans illustrates the difference between causal and institutional force in terms of a historical royal decree. If we say that this decree "took effect on August 1st, 1641," this might suggest that the decree took effect by causal force. But in fact whether the royal decree "took effect" depends on "its success in being a decree, its not being null and void; its taking effect on August 1st means that from that day certain actions were legal, in order, . . . and other actions were not, if those actions took place."[9] Austin is the first of a succession of writers to explore conditions for the "happy" functioning of performative illocutions, including initially Evans and John Searle. He distinguishes such utterances from statements, although they often presuppose statements. He carefully classifies different reasons for their failing to constitute valid illocutions, and also classifies different types of performative utterances. We explore this in due course.

Although we shall discuss whether certain types of prayer can possibly be regarded as speech acts, inspired by God, the promises of God are undoubtedly speech acts. In Genesis the divine promise to Abraham stands firm, in spite of setbacks. God has promised a child to Abraham and Sarah; thus, in Kierkegaard's language, Abraham "cannot" slay the son of promise (Gen 22). Israel's bondage in Egypt "must" issue in deliverance (Exod 6:6). David brings success after setbacks in the settlement of Canaan (2 Sam 5). *But*

---

8. Austin, *How to Do Things with Words*, 120 (his italics).
9. Evans, *The Logic of Self-Involvement*, 72.

Introduction

the covenant is always the context of effective promise. Covenant is the "institutional backing" for the performative power of God's promise. Hence Paul affirms, "In him [Christ] every one of God's promises is 'Yes'" (2 Cor 1:20). Those who believe in Jesus Christ "are descendants of Abraham" (Gal 3:7). Promise is the theme of Rom 9:4, and Heb 9:15–18 shows that the basis of effective promise is covenant.

The precise status of different types of prayer is much more complex. Vriezen considers the example of intercessory prayer in the Old Testament.[10] He admits, "We frequently find that an intercession is not, or not wholly, successful: in spite of his intercession and in spite of the fact that God responds to his appeal Abraham could not save the town (Gen 18); even though he risks his own life. Moses cannot obtain full atonement from God (Exod 32:30–35). In the case of Amos the opposite happens." First God listens to him and answers his intercession (Amos 7:1–6); but afterwards the plague must come after all (7:7–9; 8:1–3). We shall explore the vicissitudes of intercessory prayer in due course. There are, however, sufficient similarities and contrasts to consider the promises of God and divinely inspired prayer at the same time. We begin, however, with the simpler category of God's promise.

One point about prayer, however, is clear. Immanuel Kant, the philosopher, distinguished between what he called "purely rational" prayer and "churchly" prayer. In his view, rational prayer was never prayer for things to happen, it concerned only the moral stance of the one who prayed. We shall see in due course that while prayer does indeed entail the moral stance and self-involvement of the one who prays, what Kant calls "churchly" prayer and we call "biblical" prayer remains utterly central to the nature of prayer. Vincent Brümmer calls Kant's "purely rational" prayer only "therapeutic meditation," and links it to any "non-objective" conception of God, such as we find in the works of Don Cupitt.[11] We shall explore this issue further.

---

10. Vriezen, *An Outline of Old Testament Theology*, 294–95.
11. Brümmer, *What Are We Doing When We Pray?* 21 and 25.

Promise and Prayer

Meanwhile, we may note that Thomas Aquinas regarded prayer in its various traditional forms (i.e., adoration, confession, petition, and intercession) as "spoken reason (*oris ratio*)," as well as the ascent of the soul.[12] He defined prayer as "an act of reason."[13] He also regarded it as not simply the cry of human creatures to God, but "the Spirit asketh for us (Rom 8:26)."[14] Thus, like Paul, he anticipated our key point about prayer as "Divine dialogue," and saw virtually all prayer as rational as well as personal, often public and corporate, and spiritual.

---

12. Aquinas, *Summa Theologiae*, 2:2, question 83, article 1; also Jeremy Taylor, *Rule and Exercises of Holy Living*, ch. 4.

13. Aquinas, *Summa* 2:2, question 83, article 10.

14. Aquinas, *Summa* 2:2, question 83, article 10. I.e., the Spirit asks God for the things we need.

PART I

Promise in the Biblical Writings

1

Promise as a Speech Act

1. The distinctive nature of promise as a speech act: it changes a situation

A PROMISE CONSTITUTES MORE than a descriptive statement. Statements or assertions *reflect* or *describe* the world. Valid promises *change* or *transform* situations within the world. This is because in their very speaking they perform *acts:* the act of making a promise. As Austin, Evans, Searle, Recanati, Ricoeur, and many others point out, they perform an act that entails a *commitment* and a taking of responsibility. Searle calls them speech acts; Austin calls them performatives. As I wrote nearly thirty years ago, "The speaker 'stands behind' the words giving a pledge and personal backing that he or she is prepared to undertake commitments and responsibilities that are entailed in extra-linguistic terms by the proposition which is asserted."[1]

This categorizes "promise" under the heading of *speech acts*. But what does this say about the promises *of God*? When God makes a promise, God performs an act *in* the very making of a promise. It is genuinely remarkable that God makes promises at all. He voluntarily and in sovereign grace *commits* himself, or

---

1. Thiselton, *New Horizons in Hermeneutics*, 617.

Part I: Promise in the Biblical Writings

binds himself, or limits his options, to act only in accordance with what he has promised.

Hence, Austin calls these commissive performative utterances. Searle calls them commissive speech acts. We know all too well in everyday life how costly a promise can be. If God has promised to save, he cannot condemn. An invitation to a wonderful event may come after we have promised to take our son to a football match. Both Austin and Searle call such speech acts "commissives" because they are speech acts that involve commitments, which tie our hands. We have promised to undertake appropriate actions. To ascribe such self-chosen limitations to God might seem incredible, but for the fact that he has limited himself in *the covenant*.

Before making the claim that the covenant is the institution that underlies and makes possible divine promise, we must first take a step back since biblical covenants are themselves examples of promises. Clearly according to the narrator in Genesis, God could promise life or death to Adam before any covenant was enacted. Yet covenant places divine promise on a *formal* or quasi-legal setting. When God promises something happens, and the covenant gives substance to this. The covenant may indeed take the form of a promise, but of *a promise that is paradigmatic for other promises*. This is because, as Walter Eichrodt declares, a human being knows where he or she stands according to the terms revealed in the covenant: "With this God men know exactly where they stand; *an atmosphere of trust and security is created*, in which they find both the strength for a willing surrender to the will of God and joyful courage to grapple with the problems of life."[2] By contrast, the worshippers of pagan deities remained in constant fear of the arbitrariness of their supposed gods.

John Searle therefore calls this kind of thing "an institutional fact,"[3] i.e., one that applies to an institution or a corporate relationship. It stands in contrast to what he calls "a brute fact." He continues, "It is only given such institutions as the church, the law, private property, the state, and the special position of the speaker

---

2. Eichrodt, *The Theology of the Old Testament*, Vol. 1, 38 (his italics).

3. Searle, *Speech Acts*, 50–71; and Searle, *Expression and Meaning*, 1–29.

and hero within these institutions that one can excommunicate, appoint, give and bequeath one's possessions or declare war."[4]

We are now in a position to say that *the covenant is the institution that underlies divine promise*. In the covenant God promises to act in certain ways so that people know where they stand with God. In the Bible this means the covenant (the institution) of the divine King (the one with the appropriate status and role to make a covenant), ratified by sacrificial blood (the means of making a covenant); in the New Testament it means ratification by the blood of Jesus Christ.

For our purposes the most important feature of speech acts is that they *change* the world, or situations within the world, in contrast to propositions or assertions, which *describe* and reflect the world. Searle illustrates this "*difference of fit,*" as he calls this, between words and the world by citing an illustration of everyday shopping suggested by the philosopher Elizabeth Anscombe.[5] A man goes into a supermarket with a shopping list given him by his wife. He considers the list, and takes from the shelves, beans, butter, bacon, and bread. Suppose that he is followed by a store detective who writes down everything that he buys. The shopper's list and the detective's list contain the same propositional *content*; but the *force* of each list is different: the shopper's list *changes* the situation; the detective's list only *describes and reports* what is happening. Dietmar Neufeld writes, "The texts [in speech acts] are *effective acts* which change situations in the public domain in terms of . . . the consequent life-style adopted."[6]

Speech acts, of which promise constitutes a paradigm case, change the situation or the world; mere statement does not.[7] Evans, Searle, Bach and Harnish, Vanderveken, Recanati, Tsohatzidis,

---

4. Searle, *Expression and Meaning*, 18.
5. Searle, *Expression and Meaning*, 3–5, 14–16, and 18–20.
6. Neufeld, *Reconceiving Texts as Speech Acts*, ix (his italics).
7. Thiselton, "The Paradigm of Biblical Promise." Cf. Evans, *The Logic of Self-Involvement*; Bach and Harnish, *Linguistic Communication and Speech Acts*; Vanderveken, *Foundations of Illocutionary Logic*; Recanati, *Meaning and Force*; Neufeld, *Reconceiving Texts as Speech Acts*; Briggs, *Words in Action*.

Part I: Promise in the Biblical Writings

Wolterstorff, Neufeld, and Briggs are exponents of speech-act theory, after Austin and Searle, who all stress the distinctiveness of promises as speech acts.[8] This list of eight writers is certainly not exhaustive.

In the case of *God's* promises in the biblical writings there is a further difference that is distinctive to promise. This is the future or eschatological dimension noted by Moltmann, Pannenberg, Gerhard von Rad, and others. Whereas statements may describe the world as it is, promises often even contradict present states of affairs in the light of a future destined end promised by God. As Moltmann writes, "Promise must stand in contradiction to the reality which can at present be experienced. . . . [Promises] do not seek to make a mental picture of existing reality, but to lead existing reality towards the promised and hoped-for transformation."[9] Faith, led by hope and promise, he adds, stands in contrast to despair and presumption.

Moltmann writes, "Presumption is a premature, self-willed anticipation of the fulfilment of what we hope for from God. Despair is the premature, arbitrary anticipation of the non-fulfilment of what we hope for from God. Both forms of hopelessness, by anticipating the fulfilment or by giving up hope, cancel the wayfaring character hope. They rebel against the patience in which hope trusts in God of the promise."[10]

One more thing may be said about promises. They are more multitudinous in Scripture than we might imagine, because many promises do not explicitly use the language of "promise." It is no less a promise when Jesus says, "I will be with you always" (Matt 11:25) or "Whoever has faith in me shall live" (John 11:25). These are promises despite being implicit. It is conventional since Austin to speak of "implicit performatives" and implicit promises.

---

8. Evans, *The Logic of Self-Involvement*; Bach and Harnish, *Linguistic Communication and Speech Acts*; Vanderveken, *Foundations of Illocutionary Logic*; Recanati, *Meaning and Force*; Tsohatzidis (ed.), *Foundations of Speech-Act Theory*; Wolterstorff, *Divine Discourse*.

9. Moltmann, *Theology of Hope*, 18.

10. Moltmann, *Theology of Hope*, 23.

2. Promise as speech act: an alternative explanation to "word magic"

We can return now to the logic of promise. Austin brackets together, as acts of commitment, promise, covenant, give my word, pledge myself, guarantee, dedicate myself to, and to vow.[11] He also considers the speech act of blessing. Austin calls these "behabitives" (speech acts by which an attitude is adopted).

This greatly curtails premature claims about "word-magic." These arise, for example, when in Genesis Jacob cannot recall his blessing (Gen 27:33, 37), or in Numbers when Balaam tells Balak, "I have received a command to bless; he has blessed and I cannot revoke it" (Num 23:20). The reason why in Genesis and Numbers blessings cannot be recalled is because *no institutional mechanism existed to undo or revoke this speech act*. It is as if today a person might wonder why we cannot say to a baptized person who has second thoughts, "I unbaptize you." There is no institutional means of unbaptizing people.

This has nothing to do with the supposed power of words, an idea mistakenly emphasized by Grether in 1934, by Dürr in 1938, and more recently by Gerhard von Rad, W. Zimmerli, and E. Jacob.[12] Grether compared the word in the Old Testament to a missile with a time-fuse; Dürr described it as a power-laden (*kraftgeladen*) force; von Rad regarded it as "an objective reality endowed with mysterious power," and Jacob described it as "a projectile shot into the enemy camp whose explosion must sometimes be awaited but which is always inevitable."[13] But the problem of a spoken word lay in its speech-act nature: often there was no conventional procedure for recalling such a word.

---

11. Austin, *How to Do Things*, 157.

12. See Thiselton, "The Supposed Power of Words in the Biblical Writings"; Grether, *Name und Wort Gottes im Alten Testament*, especially 103–7; Dürr, *Die Wertung des göttlichen Wortes im Alten Testament*, especially 52, 61, and 71; von Rad, *Old Testament Theology*, 85; Zimmerli, "Wort Gottes" col. 1810; Jacob, *Theology of the Old Testament*, 131.

13. References are given above, in n.24.

Part I: Promise in the Biblical Writings

In my 1974 article on this issue, I considered four points that had been used to provide supposed credibility to the older theory about the power of word. First, claims were made on the basis of the fact that the Hebrew term *dābār* (word) could and did also mean *thing*. J. Pedersen, E. Jacob, and G. A. F. Knight all made questionable use of this semantic accident. Knight writes, "Once a word, *dābār*, is uttered with intent . . . it becomes a thing," like words in a speech bubble in a comic; "It has now become impossible to push these words back into the speaker's mouth. They are potent in themselves."[14] But James Barr rightly points out that this view is based on a misunderstanding of the nature of polysemy in language.[15] The sense of "word" and "thing," he says, are *alternatives*. An ancient speaker did not mean *both* senses of *dābār* when uttering the word. Consider the words "taste" in English, "Geschmack" in German, or "gusto" in Italian, which can all be applied to both food and art. This does not suggest that English, German, or Italian speakers could not distinguish between taste in the dining room and taste in the art gallery. Specialists in linguistics and semantics confirm Barr's point.[16]

The second argument is simply that we cannot generalize from force speech uttered by God or a king to words-in-general, or to any particular word. Divine words may be "power-laden" for a quite different reason than "word-magic." Most of Dürr's examples are taken from Divine discourse or are words spoken with kingly authority. Similarly, in Isa 55:10–11 it is precisely *Divine* words that shall not return empty, not words-in-general. Jeremiah 23:29 may describe a word as a hammer-blow, but this is precisely because it is *God* who speaks in judgment.

Third, it also misleading to generalize about words-in-general from specific examples of blessings and cursings. These examples are, for J. L. Austin, primary examples of performative utterances,

---

14. Knight, *A Christian Theology of the Old Testament*, 59; Knight, *A Biblical Approach to the Doctrine of the Trinity*, 14–16.

15. Barr, *The Semantics of Biblical Language*, 133–38.

16. Lyons, *Introduction to Theoretical Linguistics*, 44–45; Ullmann, *Principles of Semantics*, 114–25 and 174–80.

Promise as a Speech Act

like appointing, betting, giving and bequeathing, naming a ship, or saying, "I do" in a marriage service. Even such words do not have "power" by causal or "brute" force; they are given a special place by *institutions and conventions*. Illocutions rest on entitlements or quasi-legal status, not brute force. Clearly if no such institution or convention exists, no such force will be applicable. Jacob cannot recall his blessing once given, but not because it was "power-laden."

Fourth, too often in this debate "dynamic" language was set over against more "static" language, as if every utterance had to count as one or the other. But, as Wittgenstein insisted, we need "a radical break from the idea that language functions in one way, always serves the same purpose; to convey thoughts."[17] The functions of words, he said, are as diverse as the functions of a box of tools.[18] To bracket an argument about the supposed power of word with the need to recognize what is "dynamic" in language is to confuse two quite different things. Philosophers and experts in linguistics have long ago left behind such simplistic assumptions about language.

3. Institutional, not causal, force; and explicit and implicit speech acts

Alexandra Brown calls 1 Cor 1:18 and 2:2–5 a speech act, noting that Paul's appeal to the word of God as power is precisely *not* that of *rhetorical* persuasion.[19] Rhetorical persuasion would count as *causal* force, not institutional force, as in Austin's "perlocutions." He defines perlocutions as persuading *by* saying something, in contrast to performative "illocutions," which constitute a performative act *in* saying something.[20]

Austin carefully considers also the difference between explicit and implicit performatives. The fact that implicit forms may be

---

17. Wittgenstein, *Philosophical Investigations*, sect. 304.
18. Wittgenstein, *Philosophical Investigations*, sects. 1–37, 43, 49, 65–67, and 108.
19. Brown, *The Cross and Human Transformation*, 15–20.
20. Austin, *How to Do Things with Words*, 120–31.

Part I: Promise in the Biblical Writings

used makes criteria based on grammar or vocabulary impossible.[21] An apparent speech act of promise proves to be not one at all when someone makes a promise for us on our behalf; Austin offers the example of a parent's saying, "He promises, don't you, Willie?"[22] That utterance is not a promise. On the other hand, a promise may simply be implied, by, for example, saying "I'll be there" in place of "I promise to be there."[23] He contrasts "explicit performatives" with "primary performatives." But "primary performatives" may be ambiguous. For example, if someone shouts out, "Thunder!" this could count as a warning, a piece of information, or a prediction.[24] If the shouted acclamation functions as warning, this may be equivalent to the speech act, "I warn you to leave." A prediction might be a weaker speech act. But the shout alone would be ambiguous. By contrast, he comments, "The explicit performative rules out equivocation."[25] This helps us to avoid a particular criticism from Searle that Austin confuses particular *verbs* with specific *acts* of performative force. In his list of "commissives," Austin includes "promise," "give my word," "guarantee," "pledge myself," "bind myself," "swear," "vow," and "covenant," but he also includes "mean to," "plan," "adopt," "agree," "contemplate," etc., which lean towards "primary" performatives, which are more ambiguous.[26]

When we consider biblical examples, we shall need to consult Greek and Hebrew concordances and lexica. As we noted earlier, words can have different senses in different contexts ("taste" in the art gallery and the restaurant; "bank" by a river with a vault). The Hebrew word rendered as "promise" in English is sometimes *āmar*, usually meaning simply "say" or "said." Similarly, if we consult the Greek-English index of *The Analytical Concordance to the NRSV of the New Testament*, we find that *epaggelia*, promise, is translated fifty times as "promise," and once as "consent." The verb

21. Austin, *How to Do Things with Words*, 44–45.
22. Austin, *How to Do Things with Words*, 63.
23. Austin, *How to Do Things with Words*, 69.
24. Austin, *How to Do Things with Words*, 72.
25. Austin, *How to Do Things with Words*, 76.
26. Austin, *How to Do Things with Words*, 156–58.

Promise as a Speech Act

form, *epaggellomai*, is translated eleven times as "promise"; twice as "make a promise," and twice as "profess."[27]

If we consider "promise" in the main concordance, however, in Matt 14:7, "He *promised* on oath to grant her," the Greek word translated as "promise" is *homologeō* (usually "to confess"); in Luke 1:72, "He has shown the mercy *promised to* our ancestors" is rendered in Greek simply by *meta* ("with"); and in Acts 13:34, "Give you the holy *promises* made to David," which is rendered in Greek by *pistos* ("faithful"). On the other hand, admittedly the remaining sixty or more references reflect the normal Greek words for "a promise" (noun) or "he promises" (verb).

The most explicit performatives are often marked by a formal declaration, such as an oath. In Heb 6:13, 16, and 7:21, promising with an oath formalizes the commitment made in acts of promise. Yet an oath is not usually necessary. Some of the most paradigmatic New Testament examples of divine promise include: Rom 4:20–21, "No distrust made him [Abraham] waver concerning the promise of God . . . being fully convinced that God was able to do what he had promised"; Gal 3:16, "Now the promises were made to Abraham"; Heb 6:15, "Abraham obtained the promise"; and Heb 11:11, "he [Abraham] considered him faithful who had promised." Romans, Galatians, and Hebrews, all refer to the paradigm case of God's promise to Abraham.

At this point we should prepare the way for a deeper understanding of "institutional facts" and performative (as opposed to causal) or illocutionary force. John Searle considers the category of speech acts that he calls *directives*. These perform a "words-to-world" function. As we have said, he comments, "There must exist an extra-linguistic institution and the speaker and hearer must occupy special places within this institution."[28] He then cites such institutions as the church, the law, private property, the state, and a special position of the speaker and hearer within these institutions. He gives such examples as appointing, giving and bequeathing

---

27. Whitaker and Kohlenberger III, *The Analytical Concordance to the NRSV of the New Testament*, 740.

28. Searle, *Expression and Meaning*, 18.

one's possessions, and declaring war. We have quoted this passage in Searle before, but do so again to explain why the biblical covenants emphatically count as relevant "institutions" alongside the church, the law, and the state. This is fundamental to our discussion of promisers in the biblical writings. Dieter Neufeld, we shall see, applies the principle also to early Christian confessions of belief such as we have in 1 John. He writes, "What is confessed [i.e., key beliefs about Jesus] implies certain commitments and becomes operative in acts of communion and acts of love."[29]

In chapter 9 we shall discuss Neufeld's arguments further, comparing the more commissive or directive speech-act theory of Briggs and Neufeld with the more conversational approaches of White and Botha. The difference of approach, however, can be traced back to a possible ambiguity in Austin, where he deliberately includes what he calls "constatives" within the category of performative utterances or speech acts. The inclusion of constatives throws open the boundary of performatives so widely that it becomes difficult still to find adequate defining characteristics of performatives.

Shortly after the publication of *How to do Things with Words* a number of philosophers published a Symposium on J. L. Austin under the editorship of K. T. Fann, in which several writers made this point about the ambiguity in his work.[30] Contributors included Urmson, Warnock, Hampshire, Searle, Strawson, and two dozen more. J. O. Urmson was one of his editors and admirers, but even he remarked, "Austin . . . found it impossible to give satisfactory criteria for distinguishing the performative from other utterances."[31] He argues further "The constative seemed to collapse into the performative. . . . The various forms of constatives—stating, reporting, asserting, and the rest—seem to be merely a subgroup of performatives."[32]

---

29. Neufeld, *Reconceiving Texts as Speech Acts*, ix.
30. Fann (ed.), *Symposium on J. L. Austin*.
31. Urmson, "Austin's Philosophy," 27; cf. 22–32.
32. Urmson, "Austin's Philosophy," 27.

Promise as a Speech Act

This might not seem so serious, had not Austin begun *How to Do Things with Words* by drawing distinctions between statement and words such as "promise," "warn," "appoint," and so on. He used the term "constative" to denote "true or false" statements, which might not be descriptions.[33] Later in this book, he makes this clear by adding "expositives" to his four categories on "behabitives," "commissives," "verdictives," and "exercitives."[34] Austin admitted, "Exercitives are difficult to define."[35] How exactly do they constitute performative utterances or speech acts. Is it to make a statement, doing something or performing an act? Austin offers such examples as "I reply," "I argue," "I concede," "I illustrate," "I assume," and "I postulate."[36]

Austin actually acknowledges that these include a "marginal of awkward cases, or overlaps."[37] Indeed, that is what they are, for intuitively we want to agree that these are more than brute-fact-stating utterances. However, Urmson also recognizes that the border between illocutionary utterances and perlocutionary utterances also becomes blurred.[38] So can Austin sustain the argument that they constitute performative utterances or speech acts?

Walter Cerf is just as critical as Urmson. He writes, "As soon as Austin has established the apparently clear-cut distinction between constatives and performatives, he proceeds to show that the distinction breaks down."[39] This dilemma will bedevil argument until our final chapter when we distinguish between Briggs and Neufeld, who expound speech acts proper (or commissive speech acts) for biblical studies, and White and Botha, who expound speech acts in biblical studies more loosely. Meanwhile we are on firmer ground when we turn to promise and promising in the

---

33. Austin, *How to Do Things with Words*, 3.
34. Austin, *How to Do Things with Words*, 150–61.
35. Austin, *How to Do Things with Words*, 151.
36. Austin, *How to Do Things with Words*, 151.
37. Austin, *How to Do Things with Words*, 151.
38. Urmson, "Austin's Philosophy," 29.
39. Cerf, "Critical Review of *How to Do Things with Words*," 353; cf. 351–79.

Part I: Promise in the Biblical Writings

biblical writings, which are essentially commissives, or speech acts of commitment.

2

Promises of God in the Old Testament

GERHARD VON RAD DECLARES, "From Abraham to Malachi, Israel was kept constantly in motion because of what God said and did. . . . She was always in one way or another in an area of tension constituted by promise and fulfilment."[1] Neufeld observes that in the case of speech acts, "[t]he text's language is firmly anchored in the extra-textual historical milieu and provides the referential context through which the original meaning and the intention of the author may be recovered."[2] Many prophets echo David's words, "The promise of the LORD proves true" (2 Sam 22:31). The Psalmist declares, "The promises of the LORD are promises that are pure" (Ps 12:6). The fulfilment of promise is important. Thus, on completion of the temple, Solomon says, "Now the LORD has fulfilled his promise that he made" (2 Chr 6:10). The Psalmist again says, "This is my comfort in my distress, that your promise gives me life" (Ps 119:50). He seeks to awake early "that I may meditate on your promise" (119:148).

---

1. Von Rad, *Old Testament Theology*, Vol. 2, 371; cf. Haffemann, "Promise," 69; cf. 68–74.

2. Neufeld, *Reconceiving Texts as Speech Acts*, 2.

Part I: Promise in the Biblical Writings

1. God's promise to Abraham

Even prior to Abraham God establishes a covenant with Noah and made a promise that depended on the covenant (Gen 8:21—9:17). Concerning the figure of Abraham, Old Testament writers refer to Abraham more than forty times, and New Testament writers more than seventy times.[3] The narrative account of Abraham in Genesis continues from 11:26 to 25:18. He was born in Ur of the Chaldees, near the Euphrates in modern Southern Iraq. When he was seventy-five, God called him to travel to Canaan (some 600 miles) with Sarah, Lot, and their possessions (Gen 11:31—12:5). God's words, "I will make of you a great nation, and I will bless you" (12:2; cf. 17:4) constitutes an implicit promise. In other words, it is a promise even though the word "promise" is not used. Abraham then migrated to Shechem and Bethel, which was a further 400 miles (12:6, 8). After a sojourn in Egypt because of famine, God renewed his promises to Abraham in 13:15, "All the land you see I will give to you and to your offspring forever. I will make your offspring like the dust of the earth [i.e. countless]." Again, this is an implicit but unmistakable promise. Abraham's response was to build an altar to the LORD (13:18).

Genesis 14 recounts his meeting with the four kings and his blessing from Melchizedek (14:17-20), to whom Abraham gave tithes, and to which Hebrews alludes (Heb 7:1-10). Genesis 15 repeats God's promise of heirs (15:5) and Abraham's response of faith, which God "Reckoned . . . as righteousness" (15:6). In v. 8 he asks, in the light of a delay of some ten years, for a proof that God will indeed actualize his promise. There follows the dramatic narration of "the cutting" of the covenant with Abraham, in which a flaming torch passed between the cut pieces of a sacrifice (v. 17). (In Hebrew the making of a covenant may be described as the *"cutting"* of the covenant.) "On that day the LORD made a covenant

---

3. For a very detailed treatment of Abraham, see Morgan-Wynne, *Abraham in the Old Testament and Early Judaism*; and Morgan-Wynne, *Abraham in the New Testament*.

Promises of God in the Old Testament

with Abraham, saying, 'To your descendants I give this land'" (15:18). Once again, the promise is implicit, not explicit.

Genesis 16 recounts the narrative of Abraham, Sarah, Hagar, and Ishmael, culminating in a further solemn covenant in 17:1–8, and his name was changed to Abraham in place of Abram. This time God required a "sign" on Abraham's part, and the *institution of circumcision* is introduced (17:11–14). Genesis 18 relates the theophany at Mamre and a renewed promise (vv. 17–19), with Abraham's intercession for Sodom and Gomorrah, and for Lot. In Genesis 20 Abimelech increased Abraham's wealth. Finally in 21:1–2, "The LORD dealt with Sarah as he had said, and . . . as he had promised. Sarah conceived and bore Abraham a son in his old age." Abraham was as old as one hundred and Sarah was past the normal years of childbearing. The rest of chapter 21 concerns a treaty with Abimelech and the fate of Hagar. Genesis 22 concerns the great test of Abraham "to slay the son of promise," as Kierkegaard expressed it. Kierkegaard narrates an unforgettable picture of Abraham torn by God's command in the light of God's promise.[4] The Genesis narrative from chapters 11 to 22 gives us a picture of the crucial importance of promise, often unresolved promise, the role of covenant and covenant signs, and of Abraham's faithful responses in prayer.

From the time of Abraham onwards through Moses and the time of the conquest of Canaan God's promises often concerned the land of Canaan. In Gen 17:8 God said to Abraham, "I will give to you, and to your offspring after you, the land where you are now an alien, all the land of Canaan, for a perpetual holding; and I will be their God." The next verses appeal to the covenant (Gen 17:9–10). Thus, the territory became known as "the promised land." God then renewed the promise to Moses: "I declare that I will bring you up out of the misery of Egypt to the land of the Canaanites, the Hittites, the Amorites, . . . and the Jebusites, a land flowing with milk and honey" (Exod 3:17). Deuteronomy 34:4 repeats the promise: "The LORD said to him [i.e., Moses in his last days], 'This is the land of which I swore to Abraham, to Isaac, and

---

4. Kierkegaard, *Fear and Trembling*.

Part I: Promise in the Biblical Writings

to Jacob, saying, "I will give it to your descendants." The promise of the land is then renewed to Joshua: "Every place that the sole of your foot will tread upon I have given to you" (Josh 1:3). The past tense is an example of the prophetic perfect, denoting certainty rather than timing. In 1 Chronicles David looks back with thanksgiving to God's fulfilment of his promises and to "the covenant that he made with Abraham, his sworn promise to Isaac, which he confirmed to Jacob as a statute, and to Israel as an everlasting covenant, saying 'To you I will give the land of Canaan as your portion for an inheritance'" (1 Chr 16:16–17).

In the New Testament, one of the earliest references to the promises to Abraham is spoken by Mary in the Magnificat: "He [God] has helped his servant Israel . . . according to the promise made to our ancestors, to Abraham and to his descendants for ever" (Luke 1:55). Shortly afterwards, Zechariah, the father of John the Baptist says, "He [God] has shown the mercy promised to our ancestors, and has remembered his covenant, the oath that he swore to our ancestor Abraham, to grant us, that we . . . might serve him without fear" (Luke 1:72). The promise here in 4:13 is explicit and formally confirmed by an oath with the institution of the covenant. God's promise to Abraham occurs in Peter's speech in Acts 3:25, with reference to the covenant, and in Stephen's speech in Acts 7:17.

In the Pauline epistles a reference appears in Rom 4:3 and 9, "Abraham believed God and it was reckoned to him as righteousness," and more explicitly as promise in 4:13, "The promise that he [Abraham] would inherit the world." Paul anticipates this in Gal 3:6 and 16, "Abraham believed God . . . . The promises were made to Abraham and his offspring." Hebrews 6:13 has "When God made a promise to Abraham" with an elaborate addition about God's oath (6:13–18), and a further comment on Abraham and Melchizedek (7:1–10). By now the full nature of God's promise has become clear. It is a pledge and a binding commitment, with blessings to the recipient, mediated by the covenant (and in the New Testament by the death of Christ) and usually conveying an inheritance to heirs.

2. The promises of God to Moses, Joshua, David, Israel, and Ezekiel

The earliest reference to a covenant is in a promise made to Noah in Gen 9:11. In Exod 6:2-8 God spells out his intention to fulfil his promises made to Abraham, Isaac, and Jacob. He then adds another promise: "I will free you from the burdens of the Egyptians" (v. 6). In Exod 19:5-6 God promises, "You shall be for me a priestly kingdom and a holy nation." Yet shortly after Israel's escape from Egypt, their sin of worshipping the Golden Calf threatened to destroy their confidence in God's promise. Yet through the intercession of Moses God's promise was renewed. Moses prayed, "Remember Abraham, Isaac, and Jacob, your servants, how you swore to them by your own self" (Exod 32:13). In the advance to, and settlement of, Canaan in Joshua and Judges God's promises are renewed. "Every place that the sole of your foot will tread upon I have given to you, as I promised to Moses" (Josh 1:3). "As I was with Moses, so I will be with you" (1:5). "Be strong and courageous . . . for the LORD your God is with you . . . to take possession of the land that the LORD your God gives you to possess" (1:9, 11).

Martin Noth considers the "re-presentation" on Old Testament promises in the light of the "today" of Deuteronomy.[5] When future generations of Israelite children ask what is the meaning of the ordinances, they shall be answered: "We were Pharaoh's slaves in Egypt; and Yahweh brought us out of Egypt with a strong hand . . ." (Deut 6:20-21, Noth's translation). He compares similarly: "Today if ye will hear his voice, harden not your heart, as at Meribah, as in the day of Massah in the wilderness" (Ps 95:7-8, Noth's translation). This emphatic "today" reflects "re-presentation."

At the close of his life Joshua gave this testimony: "that not one good thing has failed of all the good things that the LORD your God has promised concerning you" (Josh 23:14). In the battle with the Philistines in 1 Samuel, in the successes of David (2 Sam 5:6-10 and 17-25), and in the settled prosperity under Solomon

---

5. Noth, "The 'Re-presentation' of the Old Testament in Proclamation," 83; cf. 76-88.

Part I: Promise in the Biblical Writings

(1 Kgs 4:20—10:29), Israel relied on God's promises. In 2 Sam 7 a new promise was offered to David concerning the throne in Jerusalem. David had at first hoped that he would build a house for the LORD, but God promised this privilege to his son, Solomon. Through Nathan, God promises, "I will make for you a great name ... and I will appoint a place for my people Israel" (2 Sam 7:9, 10). "I will establish the throne of his kingdom" (7:13). "Your house and your kingdom shall be made sure forever" (7:16).

Leviticus and Deuteronomy elaborate the content of God's promises to a faithful people in the form of a series of blessings. But should promises be rescinded because the people were faithless? Leviticus 26:40–41 affirms the possibility of repentance. There is still the possibility of hope. (We consider this issue further under heading 4, below.)

The eighth-century prophets witness to Israel's failure to live up to its responses in the covenant. Amos 3:1–2, says, "You only have I known of all the families of the earth; therefore I will punish you for all your iniquities." At first punishment did not seem to revoke God's ultimate promises. But in the late eighth century the Northern kingdom of Israel fell and in 587 B.C. the temple was destroyed and the Davidic dynasty came to an end. Psalm 77:8–9 asks about God's promises: "Has his steadfast love ceased for ever? Are his promises at an end for all time? Has God forgotten to be gracious? Has he in anger shut up his compassion?" Yet the Psalms do not seem to speak with a single voice and may not reflect the same date in Israel's history. In Psalm 89:32–36, the writer declares, "I will punish their transgressions with a rod and their iniquity with scourges; but I will not remove from him my steadfast love or be false to my faithfulness. I will not violate my covenant or alter the word that went forth from my lips. Once and for all I have sworn by my holiness; I will not lie to David. His line will continue forever and his throne endure before me like the sun."

In the post-exilic period Ezekiel renews God's promise, but adds that "It is not for your sake, O house of Israel, ... I will sanctify my great name, ... I will sprinkle clean water upon you. ... A new heart will I give you" (36:22, 23, 25). In chapter 37 a promise of new life is given: "I will open your graves and bring you up from your graves" (37:13, 14). However we date Isa 40–55, there is a clear message of restoration. "She [Jerusalem] has served her term, her penalty is paid. . . . See, the LORD comes with might, and his arm rules for him, his reward is with him," that is, his reward is his presence (40:2, 10). "As the rain and the snow come down from heaven and do not return until they have watered the earth, . . . so shall my word be that goes out from my mouth; it shall not return to me empty, but shall accomplish that which I purpose." Here is a wonderful picture of a speech act that has unstoppable consequences. Conditions of God's promise may make it seem to falter at times, but God will stand by his commitment.

3. Implicit promises

Earlier we noted that not all biblical promises were explicit promises. One very important example of implicit promises is, "Surely I am coming soon" (Rev 22:20). 2 Peter 3:9–10 addresses the problem of apparently disappointed hope:

> The Lord is not slow about his *promise*,[6] as some think of slowness, but is patient with you, not wanting any to perish, but all to come to repentance. But the day of the Lord will come like a thief, when the heavens will pass away with a loud noise and the elements will be dissolved with fire and the earth and everything that is done on it will be disclosed.

In 1 Thess 4:13—5:11 Paul's eschatological discourse takes the form of a prediction of events, not explicit promises. It is primarily an assurance for those who grieve for those who have died. But what Paul "declares" (4:15) is derived from God's promise: "God will bring him those who have died" (4:14). The dead will not lose out on no longer being alive at the *parousia* or final coming of

---

6. Schniewind and Friedrich urge that the Gk. *epaggellō* (promise) often means simply *to indicate, to declare, or report,* among Greeks and in the Jewish world: "Various words are used [for promise] in the Masoretic text and LXX." Schniewind and Friedrich, "Epaggellō" [promise], 579.

Christ. Paul refers to "the archangel's call," "the sound of God's trumpet" (4:16), and "meeting the Lord in the air" (4:17). These are well-known eschatological metaphors, but they function as implicit promises. Paul wishes to convey what is certain. In 5:2 he alludes to "a thief in the night" from the eschatological discourses of Jesus in Matthew 24 and Mark 13. This is to indicate the sudden and unexpected nature of the fulfillment of the promise.

It is very important to keep in mind that often biblical promises are made without explicitly using the word "promise." For example, God says to Noah, "I will establish my covenant with you, that never again shall all flesh be cut off by the waters of a flood, and never again shall there be a flood to destroy the earth" (Gen 9:11). God later says of the Israelites, "I will free you from the burdens of the Egyptians" (Exod 6:6). Later we read Moses' words to God, "Remember Abraham, Isaac, and Israel, your servants, how you swore to them by your own self" (Exod 32:13). God's promises to Noah, to Abraham, and later to David may not always be explicit, but all three are covenant commitments. These constitute an institutional framework.

4. Promises that appear not to have been fulfilled

The temple was destroyed in 587 BCE, and the Davidic dynasty came to an end in the exile. Has God been unfaithful to his covenant promises? Psalm 77 expresses the dilemma: "Will the LORD spurn forever, and never again be favorable? Has his steadfast love ceased forever? Are his promises at an end for all time? Has God forgotten to be gracious? Has he in anger shut up his compassion?" (77:7–9). Artur Weiser traces the Psalmist's "crisis in his own faith" when God appears to be "wholly 'Other'"; but he concludes, "The root cause of this problem is to be found not in God's character but in man's shortcomings, his wanting to force God's providential rule to adapt itself to his own standards and to worship him according to the image which man has made for himself."[7] This

---

7. Weiser, *The Psalms*, 530–31.

implies that some of God's promises must be conditional. In terms of speech-act theory we may say that God's covenant and God's promises do not always act with causal force, but with institutional force. To remain permanently valid, various presuppositions must hold sway. In the New Testament these conditions are fulfilled vicariously by Jesus Christ and his incarnation, sacrifice on the cross, and resurrection. This in no way detracts from what Zimmerli calls "the vitality of promise."[8]

Yet other utterances from the Psalms appear to state that God's promises are forever. Psalm 89:35-36 declares, "Once and for all I have sworn by my holiness; I will not lie to David. His line will continue forever." Weiser comments, "No limits are to be set to his [God's] dominion."[9]

> The gracious will of God, which is manifested in these promises, stands firm and will not be shaken even if the bearers of these promises cease to walk in the way of responsibility and obedience, which the grace of God implies, so that God has to punish them. Human sin does not put an end to divine grace, and God's judgment is nothing else than discipline and guidance on the way to salvation. God remains faithful to himself even though men are unfaithful.[10]

How can these two poles be held together? God's discipline and guidance may bring temporary setbacks. God's promises may even lead to surprise and contingency in their way of fulfilment. Wolfhart Pannenberg expounds and affirms this theme: God is faithful, and history is one; yet fulfilments may bring surprises in how fulfilment comes.[11] Zimmerli makes several relevant comments. He says, "This talk of promise is nothing rigid or crystallized."[12] On one side, "The category of promise/fulfilment

---

8. Zimmerli, "Promise and Fulfilment," 92; cf. 69-122.

9. Weiser, *The Psalms*, 592.

10. Weiser, *The Psalms*, 592-93.

11. Pannenberg, "Redemptive Event and History"; cf. "Kerygma and History."

12. Zimmerli, "Promise and Fulfilment," 91.

serves to secure the irrevocable validity of the gift bestowed by God."[13] On the other side, "Anyone who speaks of promise and fulfilment knows of veiled purposes and distressed waiting; he knows of walking, and not only of standing still; he knows of a summoning, and not only an act of looking on. History receives a declivity toward that which is yet to come."[14] Zimmerli adds, "It is also plain that the knowledge of promise and fulfilment entails a journey, a 'being on the way.' . . . A new content emerges in the promise. In the statements of promise in the books of Kings the note of judgment and doom is sounded."[15] Part of this apparent duality is because promise is "supremely personal." "Promise develops from a prophecy of doom to prophecy of salvation."[16]

---

13. Zimmerli, "Promise and Fulfilment," 95.
14. Zimmerli, "Promise and Fulfilment," 97.
15. Zimmerli, "Promise and Fulfilment," 98 and 99.
16. Zimmerli, "Promise and Fulfilment," 105.

3

God's Promises in the New Testament

IN THE NEW TESTAMENT the promises of God no longer concern primarily possession of the land, the glorification of Jerusalem, or the prosperity of the Davidic dynasty, except in as far as these were related typologically to Jesus Christ and a heavenly "land." In general, George Guthrie writes, "The promises made to Abraham form not only the foundation of Israel's history but also the foundation of the New Testament theology of promise."[1] This shall become clear later in this chapter.

Zimmerli calls the promise in the New Testament "The New Testament message of Fulfilment" in which the word of God is fulfilled in Jesus Christ "wholly and completely." He cites Paul's words that "all promises are yea and amen" (2 Cor 1:20).[2] He points to the "today" of fulfilment in New Testament preaching, which is "once for all."[3] Christ, he says, "is the end of the old covenant and

---

1. Guthrie, "Promise," 968; cf. 967–70.
2. Zimmerli, "Promise and Fulfilment," 113.
3. Zimmerli, "Promise and Fulfilment," 114.

Part I: Promise in the Biblical Writings

its promise."[4] But, as against Bultmann, he does not strip history away from New Testament promise.[5]

In the New Testament "promise" (Greek, *epaggelia*) occurs fifty-two times: nine times in Luke-Acts, twenty-six times in the Pauline corpus, fourteen times in Hebrews, once in 1 John, and twice in 2 Peter.[6] (Almost half of references to "promise" in the New Testament occur either in Acts or Hebrews.) In Luke 24:49, as we have seen, Jesus says, "I am sending upon you what my Father promised" (i.e., the Spirit) and in Acts 1:4 he tells the apostles "to wait there [in Jerusalem] for the promise of the Father." God alone fulfils this promise. The promise is made "to our ancestors" (Acts 16:32) and to those who responded to Peter's sermon at Pentecost (Acts 2:38–39). The fulfilment of the promise becomes "good news" or the gospel (Greek, *euangelion*).

The most striking effects of God's promise concerned forgiveness of sins, salvation or eternal life, and the gift of the Holy Spirit. God had long promised the outpouring of the Spirit (Isa 44:3). Jesus promised that God would send another Counsellor (Greek, *paraklētos*), one called alongside to help (John 14:16, 26). Jesus repeats the promise in Luke 24:49: "See, I am sending upon you what my Father promised, . . . power from on high." Similarly in Acts 1:4: "He ordered them . . . to wait for the promise of the Father." Luke refers to Jesus' sending "what my Father promised," the content of which was "power from on high." Acts 2:38–39 confirms that the promise is that "You will receive the gift of the Holy Spirit" and extends the promise as "for you and for your children," and for "everyone whom the Lord calls." Paul calls this receiving

---

4. Zimmerli, "Promise and Fulfilment," 115.

5. Zimmerli, "Promise and Fulfilment," 116–20.

6. After the close of the canon, *epaggellomai* and *epaggelia* (verb and noun of "promise") occur some thirty-three times in the Apostolic Fathers. The Shepherd of Hermas speaks of promises made by one person to another (Herm. Vis. 5.2.3, and Herm. Sim. 5.2.7). But more characteristically 1 Clem. 10:2 speaks of Abraham's inheriting the promises of God. 1 Clem. 32.2 declares that the promise of God is that "your seed shall be as the stars of heaven." In 1 Clem. 27.1, 2 Clem. 15.4, and Ignatius Trallians 11.2, God is faithful to his promises. God stands by his commitments.

God's Promises in the New Testament

"the promise [of the Spirit] through faith" (Gal 3:14). In the earliest preaching the promise of God often concerned *the coming of the Holy Spirit*.

In the Gospels Jesus' gift of the Holy Spirit is associated with healing miracles and the gift of peace, extending the impact of the promise of the Spirit. Matthew 12:18–20 reads, "Here is my servant, whom I have chosen, my beloved with whom my soul is well pleased. I will put my Spirit upon him, and he will proclaim justice to the gentiles. He will not wrangle or cry aloud nor will anyone hear his voice in the streets. He will not break a bruised reed or quench a smoldering wick until he brings justice to victory." This is a quotation from Isaiah 42 and is followed by the account of the healing of the demoniac who was blind and mute (v. 23). Jesus exclaimed, "if it is by the Spirit of God that I cast out demons, then the kingdom of God has come to you" (12:28). In Luke's account of the healing of the paralytic (Luke 5:17–26) the climax is, "When he saw their faith, he [Jesus] said, 'Friend, your sins are forgiven you'" (v.20).

In Paul's writings, the continuity of his own message with Old Testament promises is acknowledged in his statement, "Abraham believed God, and it was reckoned to him as righteousness" (Rom 4:3, which exactly reflects Gen 15:6). Further, Paul writes to the Galatians, "Christ redeemed us from the curse of the law. . . . In order that in Christ Jesus the blessing of Abraham might come to the gentiles, so that we might receive the promise of the spirit through faith" (3:13–14).

Paul declares that the law of God and the promise of God are incompatible principles in Rom 4:13–14: "For the promise . . . did not come to Abraham through the law but through the righteousness of faith." In Paul the content of the promise is God's free grace.[7] The law of Moses cannot be a condition for the reception of the promise. After all, Abraham received the promise before the law was even given. His trust in God was the means by which he received the promise. The law, when it is given, does not annul the prior covenant (Gal 3:17) and the inheritance comes for "the

---

7. Hoffmann, "epagelia," 71; cf. 68–74.

Part I: Promise in the Biblical Writings

promise of God" (Gal 3:18). Paul declared that those who believe, as Abraham believed God's promise, are descendants of Abraham (Gal 3:7). "If you belong to Christ, then you are Abraham's offspring, heirs according to the promise" (Gal 3:29).[8] God's promises have been given God's "yes" in Christ (2 Cor 1:20).

So, as we have seen, promise constitutes a key concept in Paul's inclusion of the gentiles in God's blessing. If they believe the message of the gospel, as Abraham did, even without the law, they will be counted righteous. Promise also underpins his future hope for the people of Israel. In Rom 9–11 Paul struggles with the question as to whether God's promises to Israel are still valid. On the one side, he argues that to Israel belong "the adoption, the glory, the covenants, the giving of the law, worship, and the promises" (Rom 9:4). On the other side, Paul expounds the disobedience of unbelieving Jews (Rom 9:31–32; 10:3, 21). Nevertheless he cannot believe that God has given up on his promises to Israel: "I ask then has God rejected his people? By no means!" (Rom 11:1). In the biblical writings, including in Isaiah and in Paul, it seems impossible to answer clearly whether God's promises are always conditional or unconditional on human responses. In the end he declares, "The gifts and calling of God [to Israel] are irrevocable" (11:29). Yet he also admits that the paradox remains a mystery (11:33–36).[9] Paul uses the word "promise" four times in Rom 4:13–16.

The Epistle to the Hebrews interprets God's promise of "rest" in the promised land typologically: "a sabbath rest still remains for the people of God" (4:9). God is said to give "the promise of entering his rest," while the promise is still open (Heb 4:1 and 6). The promises of God in the Old Testament, the author argues, are not yet complete or fulfilled. The birth of Isaac, for example, was a partial fulfilment of God's promise to Abraham. The "rest" (Greek,

---

8. In applying God's promises to Christ-believers, Paul concludes in Romans, "It is not the children of the flesh who are the children of God, but the children of the promise are counted as descendants" (Rom 9:8).

9. This survey is confirmed by: Danker, "*epaggelia*" (promise); Gowan, "Promise"; Schniewind and Friedrich, "*epaggellō*" (promise); Louw and Nida (eds.), *Greek-English Lexicon of the New Testament Based on Semantic Domains*, 421–22; and Sand, "*epaggelia, epaggellomai, epaggelma.*"

God's Promises in the New Testament

katapausis) still remains for the people of God, which will be their eternal inheritance (Heb 9:15). The "cloud of witnesses" did not yet receive all that God promised (Heb 11:39).

Hebrews 11:8–19 interprets God's promise to Abraham typologically as for "strangers and foreigners on the earth" who looked forward to the city that has foundations, whose architect and builder is God" (11:10, 13).

The new covenant is enacted on "better promises" (Greek, *kreittōn*; Heb 8:6) than the old covenant. This leads on to the concept of "today" in *"Today* if you hear his voice," which originally comes from Ps 95:7. The fulfilment of God's promises is gradually drawing nearer (Heb 10:25). Promise and eschatology are impossible to disentangle in the New Testament.

2 Peter speaks of "very great promises," which all come to completion in Jesus Christ (2 Pet 1:3–4). All the promises of God converge in Christ; Paul was on trial for "the promise made by God to our fathers concerning the resurrection of the dead" (Acts 23:6). God's promises give rise to boldness and confidence.

Eventually the promises of God turn on eschatology: "Where is the promise of his coming?" (2 Pet 3:4). "The Lord is not slow about his promise, . . . but we wait for new heavens and a new earth" (2 Pet 3:9, 13). In the first place, this eschatological promise was made by Jesus (Matt 25:31 and Acts 1:11). James wrote that those who endure trials will receive "the crown of life which God has promised to those who love him" (Jas 1:12).

In the Epistle to the Hebrews God even confirmed his promise with a sworn oath, a procedure that greatly puzzled Philo.[10] Why should the God who is always true and faithful need to confirm his promise with an oath? This, according to Hebrews, may have been to assure other people. The writer explains, "When God desired to show even more clearly to the heirs of the promise the unchangeable character of his purpose, he guaranteed it by an oath, so that through two unchangeable things, in which it is impossible that God would prove false, we . . . might be strongly encouraged to

---

10. Philo, *de sacrificiis Abelis et Caini*, 91–94; Philo, *Legum allegoriae*, 3.203–7.

Part I: Promise in the Biblical Writings

seize the hope set before us" (Heb 6:17–18).[11] The emphasis here is on the *utter reliability* of Divine promise.

---

11. Worley, "Fleeing Two Immutable Things: God's Oath-Taking"; and Thiselton, "Hebrews," 1464; Attridge, *Epistle to the Hebrews*, 180–83; Lane, *Hebrews 1-8*, 152–53.

4

Do All Biblical Promises Apply Universally?

HUMAN PROMISES ARE SUBJECT to human frailties. This does not mean that all merely human promises are broken. Jacob exacted a promise from Joseph that he would not bury him in Egypt (Gen 47:29–30) and Joseph kept his promise (50:7–13). However, we are subject to sin and we can break promises. Moses thus commanded the Israelites to keep promises (Deut 23:23) and warned them of consequences if they broke their promises (Num 32:24). Balak made a promise to Balaam that proved futile (Num 12:17). Haman made a promise that was wicked, and eventually was hanged (Esth 4:7). In the Gospels, the chief priests promised to give money to Judas (Mark 14:11). Promising is not inherently good and keeping promises is not automatic.

When we turn to the promises of God, what may be doubted is not whether all of God's promises are utterly reliable, but the idea that every promise of God is open to universal, unconditional appropriation in any and all circumstances. What is "questionable" is not God, the promise-maker, but the human addressee of promises. *To whom* are the promises made? Part of the problem is the use of "you" in so many biblical promises. For example, very

Part I: Promise in the Biblical Writings

often the promise "When *you* pass through the waters, I will be with *you*. When *you* pass through the fire, *you* will not be burned" (Isa 43:2) is applied to *all Christians in times of doubt*. So is, "As a mother comforts her children, so I will comfort *you*" (Isa 66:13). But the former is addressed to the exiles returning from Babylon and the latter is addressed to Jerusalem, decimated by Babylonian forces. Whether this may be appropriated by all who aspire to call themselves Christians is at least worthy of consideration and cannot simply be assumed. The key question concerns timing and context. Clearly many promises are not conditional on timing and context; but some certainly are.

The classic example of the indiscriminate appropriation of God's promises can be found in what has been known since Victorian times as the "Promise Box." I do not want for one moment to devalue the help and comfort that some may have derived from this source. But it is necessary to examine its assumptions and validity as genuine personal promise. "Promise Boxes" were produced in France from about 1814 and have been produced in Britain in the nineteenth century by Pickering and Inglis, then of Glasgow. They produced "The Daily Bread Promise Box," followed by the Gospel Text, from "Line Company of Seymour, Indiana." In the 1940s Zondervan Publishers have produced the "Daily Manna Promise Box," and currently Promise Boxes can be obtained from the Dayspring Company. Conversations about Promise Boxes still occur today on the internet. Similarly promise verses are often compiled online for indiscriminate consumption. For instance, a list of fifty such texts is gathered on the Bible Study Tools website.[1] The list is headed "Let God's promises shine on your problems."

The normal practice is to use cards or slips of paper printed with Bible verses. Each day different cards or slips of paper can be drawn out of the box to discover "what message God has for me today." Normally the box yields such verses as "The peace of God which passeth all understanding shall keep your hearts and minds through Christ Jesus" (Phil 4:7; KJV/AV). This particular example was applied to all the Christian believers in Philippi

---

1. www.biblestudytools.com; accessed 12 July 2018.

Do All Biblical Promises Apply Universally?

without any contextual reasons for restricting it to them. Thus, it might plausibly be generalized for all Christians and therefore may bring valid assurance. But another popular example comes from Isa 43:2: "When you pass through the waters, I will be with you; and through the rivers, they shall not overwhelm you; when you walk through fire, you shall not be burned, and the flame shall not consume you" (NRSV). This promise was addressed to Israel returning from Babylonian exile and may or may not be universalized for all Christians in any circumstances. The fact that it would not have been applicable to all Israelites at all stages of Israel's history suggests that its application is restricted in some ways.

Another frequently used promise comes from Ps 121:8: "The LORD will keep you from all evil; your going out and your coming in from this time on and forevermore" (NRSV). It is easier to understand Isa 40:31 in a more universal context: "Those who wait for the LORD shall renew their strength, they shall mount up with wings like eagles, they shall run and not be weary, they shall walk and not faint" (NRSV). The promise to all those exiles who wait on the LORD seems open to a wider extension to God's people in other situations who wait upon him. And the clearly poetic or metaphorical language open up possibilities for less literal applications to many situations. But what of Isa 54:17: "No weapon forged against you will prevail, and you will refute every tongue that accuses you"? (NIV).

Many New Testament promises are without doubt universal. 1 John 1:9 says, "If we confess our sins, he [God] is faithful and just and will forgive our sins" (NIV). John 3:16 reads: "God so loved the world that he gave his one and only Son, that whoever believes in him shall not perish but have eternal life" (NIV). These promises have no contextual or temporal conditions. Yet many promises in the Old Testament seem to be related to a particular context and time. Deuteronomy 31:8 says, "The LORD himself goes before you and will be with you; he will never leave you nor forsake you. Do not be afraid; do not be discouraged" (NIV). This concerns Israel's entry into Canaan under Joshua. Similarly Jer 29:11 reads: "I know what plans I have for you . . . plans to prosper you and not to harm you, plans to give you hope and a future" (NIV). Jeremiah's is not a general message to everyone but a specific message to the Jewish exiles in Babylon. Its broader application cannot simply be taken for granted.

There are exceptions in both Testaments. Proverbs does seem to suggest such universal maxims as "Dishonest money dwindles away, but whoever gathers money makes it grow"; but it would be irresponsible to treat this wise observation as a mechanical blueprint for business and similar pseudo-universals. Even generalizations have to be qualified. (And, of course, in the example from Proverbs, we are talking about a maxim, rather than a divine promise as such.) Psalm 21:1 says "No one whose hope is in you [God] will ever be put to shame"—which Paul sees as having application to gentile Christians as well as Jews (Rom 10:11). So both Old and New Testaments include promises (or maxims) that have broad or even universal applicability. Similarly, both Testaments have contextually limited promises. One thinks, for example, of the story of Jesus inviting Peter to step out of the boat and walk on water (Matt 14:28–33). The implicit promise that Peter would not sink hardly constitutes some general divine promise that any Christian can "claim" for themselves.

In conclusion, when considering apparent Divine promises in Scripture, we need to be certain that they are in fact promises (as opposed to, say, a wise proverbial generalization about how things usually go) and we need to bear in mind whom they are addressed to. Some Divine promises are clearly situation- or person-specific and limited in applicability, others are clearly general promises that anyone can seek to appropriate, while yet others may be extendable to fresh situations, but such extension must be done with care and caution. Appropriating Divine promises inappropriately is a road to disappointment.

PART II

Prayer in the Biblical Writings

5

The Range of Types of Prayer in the Bible

THERE IS A DANGER that to consider prayer at this stage may blunt what we are saying more clearly about promise by distraction. Hence, we make only one preliminary point here about prayer. Immanuel Kant, the philosopher, distinguishes between two types of prayer. At first sight we might think of these as prayers of adoration and praise and prayers of intercession. But Kant means more than this. In his book *Religion within the Limits of Reason Alone* he distinguished between rational faith (*reiner Vernunftglaube*), and revealed religion as practiced in the church (*Kirchenglaube*). The first type of prayer, he argued, was broadly a mental activity in which the one who prays seeks to become aligned with God. The second type of prayer includes specific intercessory prayer that some change in circumstances will be made.[1]

In Kant's view, prayer should serve simply as a means of furthering moral religion in human beings, without what the church or popular biblical religion allegedly added. Prayer as nothing other than an aid to furthering moral religion need have no objective focus outside the human subject. Vincent Brümmer calls Kant's

---

1. Kant, *Religion within the Limits of Reason Alone*, 181.

purely "rational" prayer merely "therapeutic meditation" and cites Don Cupitt as being among those who still hold this entirely subjective view of prayer.[2]

This "subjective" form of prayer is certainly an important part of prayer. Acts of adoration, veneration, confession, and thanksgiving seem often to belong to this category. Further, the one who prays is transformed in self-involvement in praying for God's will or in adoration, confession, or thanksgiving. Thomas More (1478–1535), for instance, is credited with praying, "The things, good Lord, that I pray for, give me grace to labour for."[3] Prayer transforms the pray-er. But there is more to prayer than this.

Prayer is inter-personal. Prayer in the Bible is addressed to God who is both transcendent and immanent. Thus, thinking of God as just like a human is excluded. God says, "My ways are not your ways, neither are my thoughts your thoughts" (Isa 55:5–11). But nonetheless, the relationship remains interpersonal. Trust in the efficacy of Israel's prayer is based on assurances of God's care for Israel and his commitments through the covenant. Israelite prayer presupposes that God will hear and will respond through words and actions. Hence there are prayers of petition and intercession. There is no hint that Kant's and Cupitt's purely subjective prayer is assumed.

1. Four types of prayer

Prayer often takes the form of a request for help on behalf of others and oneself, with the expectation of an answer. From Genesis to Chronicles and in Ezra and Nehemiah prayers are embedded within narratives that indicate Divine response.[4]

---

2. Brümmer, *What Are We Doing When We Pray?* 20–21; Cupitt, *Taking Leave of God*, 68–69.

3. Thomas More, in Ashwin, *The Book of a Thousand Prayers*, 29.

4. Cf. Greeven, *"euchomai"* and *"proseuchomai"* (to pray); Newman, "Prayer"; and Miller, *They Cried to the Lord*.

The Range of Types of Prayer in the Bible

Petition

Ronald Clements has given us a useful insight into four main types of biblical prayer in his book *In Spirit and in Truth*.[5] He begins, first, with the subject of *petition*, asking *on behalf of oneself*, stating that this is one of the most basic expressions of prayer. He cites, "Ask, and it will be given you" (Luke 11:9). Many prayers in the Bible begin with asking God for things, although it is easy to see how, if petition alone is allowed to dominate all our praying, it can become self-centered and ultimately destructive of the very growth and spiritual understanding that we seek.

Intercession

Second, Clements points out that this is not the case with another form of prayer, namely *intercession*. Here we seek for things *on behalf of others*. He writes: "Undoubtedly a healthy measure of outgoing and self-giving is found in our being prepared to think about the needs and concerns of other people."[6] In empathizing with others, we are allowed a considerable personal freedom, rather than God's will and intentions being forced upon us. We are given the dignity and possibilities that our freedom represents. Petition involves a prominent element of self-discovery, but intercession requires of us a very marked willingness to discover the circumstances and needs of others.

Clements suggest that the prayer of intercession by Moses in Num 14:13–23 is one of the most outstanding examples of intercessory prayer.[7] The people of Israel had been grumbling that they would have preferred to die in Egypt or in the wilderness rather than leave Egypt under the leadership of Moses and Aaron. Now Moses says to the LORD, "Then the Egyptians will hear of it" (14:13), and will assume that Israel's God is unable to bring them out of Egypt (13:16). He thus first appeals to the name and

---

5. Clements, *In Spirit and in Truth*, 10–14.
6. Clements, *In Spirit and in Truth*, 11.
7. Clements, *In Spirit and in Truth*, 39–49, especially 44–48.

reputation of God. Then he turns to intercession: "Let the power of the LORD be great as you have promised, saying, 'The LORD is slow to anger, and abounding in steadfast love, forgiving iniquity and transgression, but by no means clearing the guilty, visiting the iniquity of the parents to the children upon the third and the fourth generation.' Pardon iniquity of this people according to the greatness of your steadfast love, just as you have pardoned this people, from Egypt even until now" (14:18–19).

Clements comments, "It would be hard to overestimate the significance of this prayer.... It displays the Israelite people in a mood that is downright shocking.... Nor does it withhold any of the most selfish, cowardly, and unworthy expressions of ingratitude and faithlessness of Israel."[8] Nevertheless, it is a prayer for forgiveness, and as such it constitutes a basic part of our vocabulary of prayer.

Confession

Third, awareness of our own need and urgency in petitions and selecting the priorities of others in our intercessions speedily brings us to the next form of prayer, which is also central in the Bible, namely *contrition and confession*. It is self-evident that the more we ask for things for ourselves and the more we ask for things for others the more we realize that the very idea about asking anything at all in prayer is filled with a boldness and assurance that borders on spiritual impertinence. Clements writes, "The expectation of establishing a communion with God through prayer raises for us an extraordinary range of thoughts and notions which relate to God's graciousness and our own unworthiness."[9]

---

8. Clements, *In Spirit and in Truth*, 47.
9. Clements, *In Spirit and in Truth*, 12.

The Range of Types of Prayer in the Bible

Praise

This brings us to a fourth form of prayer, which is ultimately the most central in biblical prayer of all. This is *praise* to God. If petition and intercession are a form of self-discovery we are even more overwhelmed by the unlimited and imaginable greatness of the creator to whom we pray. If we have done nothing more than lift our hearts to God in praise, we have achieved the greatest goal possible for any prayer. We may simply stop and let our minds contemplate God. Clements writes, "To praise God is to rethink God's thoughts."[10] With praise to God we may include thanksgiving and worship.

Miller writes, "The reference to God's greatness and the mighty hand is typical of Deuteronomy and especially in reference to the deliverance from Egypt. The word for 'greatness' here is used of God only in Deuteronomy except for one reference to God's mercy in Moses prayer in Num 14:19 and two references in the Psalms (79:11 and 150:2). In both Deut 32:3 and Ps 150:2 allusion to God's 'greatness is explicitly part of hymnic praise to God.'"[11] Deuteronomy 3:24 is even more evident: "Who is God in the heavens and on earth who can perform deeds and mighty acts like yours." But here, again, if sheer praise as such has arguably little situation-changing cognitive or evidential content, the "presupposition" of this praise (to use Evans' term) is that God has acted in ways that have changed situations.

David's declaration of praise in 2 Sam 7:18–29 is essentially like Deut 3:24, an exaltation of the greatness of God as manifest and what God has done: "O LORD God [repeated eight times in the prayer] O LORD of hosts the God of Israel, your name will be magnified for ever in the saying, 'The LORD of hosts is God over Israel.'" The observable effects of God's acts are twofold: the establishment of David and the promise of the Davidic royal line. Miller writes, "David's recitation of those two divine acts is the biblical expression of praise that declares—again like Deut. 3:24—the

10. Clements, *In Spirit and in Truth*, 13.
11. Miller, *They Cried to the Lord*, 63.

Part II: Prayer in the Biblical Writings

incomparability of God's greatness: 'Therefore you are great, for there is none like you, and there is no God besides you, according to all that we have heard with our ears' (Deut. 3:22)." Here, once again, praise is inseparably bound up with God's acts of effects in the world.

Solomon continues these acts of praise, which are connected with God's acts in the world: "O LORD, God of Israel, there is no God like you in heaven above or in the earth beneath" (1 Kgs 8:23). This dual theme continues in Jehoshaphat's prayer in the face of the Moabites and Ammonites (2 Chr 20:5-12): "Are you not God in heaven? Do you not rule over all the kingdoms of the nations? In your hand are power and might so that no one is able to withstand you. Did you not, O our God, drive out the inhabitants of this land before your people Israel, and give it for ever to the descendants of your friend Abraham?" Praise is bound up with God's observable acts of salvation in history.

2. Hebrew and Greek terms for types of prayer

These initial four forms of prayer do not of course exhaust examples of types of prayer in the biblical writings. One of the most prominent, for example, is lament or even complaint, which are abundant in the Psalms and Wisdom literature. The English word *prayer* in the biblical writings often translates the Hebrew term *tefillah* or the Greek word *proseuchē*. *Tefillah* is a general word for prayer, especially for supplication or entreaty. It may also be used for prayers of lament, which occur many times in Psalms.

The Greek term *proseuchē* may simply denote a request, but in religious texts may denote a petition to God or a vow. But some eight other words are also used, for example in Hebrew *pālal* means to pray, *chānan* means to request, *'āthar* means to entreat, *dārash Y-h-w-h* means to seek the LORD, and *qārā' bashem* means to call on the name. In addition to these *bārakh* means to bless, *hālal* means to praise, and *yādāh* means to thank or to confess.

Greek offers some seven words for prayer in a broad sense. Apart from the general word *proseuchē*, prayer, and *proseuchomai*, to pray, *deēsis* means petition, *ekzēteō* means to enquire or to seek, *aineō* means to praise, *eulogeō* means to bless, *doxazō* means to glorify, and *homologeō* means to confess, or to profess.

3. Blessing

There is still more to biblical prayer than Clements' four kinds. Consider blessing.

Blessing

Some of the earliest prayers, as we have already seen, are blessings, which may perhaps be considered a subset of intercession (when concerning humans) and of praise (when directed to God). In Gen 9:26 we see blessing as praise: Noah says, "Blessed by the LORD my God be Shem." Five chapters later, in Gen 14:19, we see blessing as intercession: Melchizedek says, "Blessed be Abraham by God Most High, Maker of heaven and earth." In Numbers the priestly blessing is a prayer: "The LORD bless you and keep you; the LORD make his face to shine upon you" (6:24–25). We argued above that blessing has nothing to do with "word magic." In Deut 28:3 "Blessed shall you be in the city and blessed shall you be in the field" is attributed to Moses as part of his prayer to God; for only God can ultimately grant blessing. In third person narrative form Ruth 2:20 recounts, "Eli would bless Elkanah his wife and say, 'May the LORD repay you with children.'" The effects of the blessing are clear: as we have argued, prayers of blessing are more than "therapeutic meditation," even if not as evidential as many petitions.

Blessing and Prediction

Sometimes prayer may seem to border on prediction or prophetic narration. This may be said of Jacob's blessing in Gen 49:2–27. Jacob prays concerning the destiny of his twelve sons. Clements interprets this blessing as predicting Israel's indebtedness of the tribes

Part II: Prayer in the Biblical Writings

of Canaan. Israel was indebted, first, to the Phoenician invention of the first alphabetic script, and thus the possibility of a greatly simplified and more versatile way of writing. Not only in recording business transactions, but in setting down myths, legends, and the records of historical events, writing was to become a cornerstone of human culture and achievement. Second, the Canaanites greatly influenced Israel in terms of techniques and skills of agriculture and an established, settled, urban pattern of life made necessary by the need to protect the cultivated soil. Third, Israel also owed much to Canaan in social and political organization. All this was foreshadowed in Jacob's blessing on his twelve sons.

The narrator writes, "Then Jacob called his sons, and said, 'Gather yourselves together that I may tell you what shall befall you in days to come. Assemble and hear, O sons of Jacob, and hearken to Israel your father.'" Jacob then enumerates characteristics and blessings concerning Rueben, Simeon and Levi (who are actually cursed rather than blessed), Judah, Zebulun, Issachar, Dan, Asher, Naphtali, Joseph, and Benjamin. Rueben is "pre-eminent in pride and pre-eminent in power" but unstable as water; Simeon and Levi are "weapons of violence"; Judah "will be on the neck of your enemies; your father's sons will bow down before you"; Zebulun shall dwell at the shore of the sea; he shall become a haven for ships, and his border shall be at Sidon. Issachar is a strong ass, crouching between the sheepfolds; Dan shall judge his people as one of the tribes of Israel. Joseph is "a fruitful bough, a fruitful bough by a spring; his branches run over the wall. . . . The God of your father will help you, God Almighty will bless you with blessings of heaven above, blessings of the deep that couches beneath, blessings of the breasts and of the womb. . . . Benjamin is a ravenous wolf, in the morning devouring the prey, and at even dividing the spoil" (Gen 49:1–27).

Like Jacob before him, Moses makes a declaration of blessing concerning Rueben, Levi, Benjamin, Joseph, Issachar, Gad, Dan, Naphtali, and Asher. He prays, for example, "May Rueben live and not die out, even though his numbers be few." Of Levi he said, "They teach Jacob your ordinances and Israel your law; they place incense before you, and whole burnt offering upon your altar." Of Benjamin he said, "The beloved of the LORD rests in safety—The High God surrounds him all the day long—the beloved rests between his shoulders." And of Joseph he said, "Blessed by the LORD be his land, with the choice gifts of heaven above, and of the deep that lies beneath." He concludes the whole prayer of blessing: "Happy are you, O Israel! Who is like you, a people saved by the LORD, the shield of your help and the sword of your triumph! Your enemies shall come fawning to you; and you shall tread upon their backs" (Deut 33:6–29; NRSV).

Clements comments on this passage: "For the most part it [the prayer] consists of affirmation and petition, the affirmation being concerned with who God is and what God has done for the people. The petition is almost entirely taken up with concern for the welfare and prosperity of the 12 separate tribes of Israel in their individual territorial holdings. . . . Behind this diversity of opportunity and experience there lies a sense of a common shared inheritance and our knowledge of one incomparable, unchanging God."[12]

Moses did not live to see the crowning indication of his leadership in bringing the Hebrew slaves out of Egypt. He died before they finally entered and settled in the promised land. In a remarkable and rather poignant comment on the death of this great leader the biblical historian simply records the fact of his death in the land of Moab and the lack of any identification of the place of his burial (Deut 34:5–6). But a biblical tradition relates how, before his death, God took Moses to the top of Mount Pisgah and showed him all the land that would eventually belong to his people and their descendants (Deut 34:1–4).

---

12. Clements, *In Spirit and in Truth*, 55.

6

Can Some Prayers Be Said to Constitute Speech Acts?

THE QUESTION THAT CONFRONTS us now is whether prayers, like promises, can be considered as speech acts. We maintain that they can, though unlike promise they form an array of different kinds of speech act rather than a single type. And these various kinds of prayer vary in their strength and weakness as speech acts. Austin and Warnock clearly imply this possibility.[1] After all, Austin included among his performative acts "to apologize" (vaguely akin to confession of sins), "thanking" (akin to thanksgiving to God), "blessing" and "congratulating" (vaguely akin to adoration or veneration), and even "deploring" (vaguely akin to repenting). All these come under his heading of "behabitives," which are certainly not "commissives."[2] In Austin's five types of performatives, his "commissives," "verdictives," and "exercitives" are "strong" speech acts, compared with his "weaker" "behabitives" and "expositives."[3]

The philosopher Geoffrey Warnock similarly argues that different speech acts vary in degree from strong to weak. The strong

1. Warnock, "Some Types of Performative Utterance."
2. Austin, *How to Do Things with Words*, 159.
3. Austin, *How to Do Things with Words*, 152–63.

Can Some Prayers Be Said to Constitute Speech Acts?

are performative speech acts, Austin concludes, but "the Behabitive is the adopting of an attitude, and the expositive is the clarifying of reasons, arguments, and communications."[4] The least that we can say as preliminary note is that both promise and prayer are deeply *inter-personal,* and in this sense concern something or someone beyond oneself. Neither promise nor prayer operate in the context of hyper-individualism or solipsism. This is exactly the point that Steven Davis makes in his essay, "Anti-Individualism and Speech Act Theory."

Promise gives us the confidence to pray. On the other hand, changes to situations do *not* uniformly come in response to every request. Some prayers go unanswered. Requests may constitute *conditions* for answers to prayer. Thus Edgar Brightman writes that even if God *always already wants "the best possible" for us* before we pray, nevertheless "*The best possible when men pray would be better than the best possible when they do not pray.* . . . God would be able to do what he could not do in the absence of that attitude [of prayer]."[5] In this sense, it is not unreasonable to say that prayer can have effects in everyday situations in the world, even if not all prayers are answered.

This sets it apart from Kant's notion of prayer as wholly "therapeutic meditation" and nothing more. Some aspects of prayer do indeed constitute therapeutic meditation, except that in the presence of God it is more than meditation. But prayer offered in faith as an act of entreaty remains nearer to constituting a speech act than to remaining only an assertion or statement. It complements the speech act of promise. Serious and sincere prayer commits the one who prays to action which is consonant with a union of wills with God. Brümmer writes, "Submitting to the authority of God entails making God's will our own and living our lives in accordance with it."[6]

---

4. Austin, *How to Do Things with Words,* 162.
5. Brightman, *A Philosophy of Religion,* 237 (my italics).
6. Brümmer, *What Are We Doing?* 61.

Part II: Prayer in the Biblical Writings

In the following chapters, we shall consider three case studies in more detail: (a) blessings, (b) thanksgiving and praise, and (c) petitions and intercessions.

7

Prayers of Blessing

Are These "Weaker" Speech Acts?

IF WE REFER TO Austin's performative utterances, we may recall Warnock's distinction between strong and weak speech acts. Austin's "behabitives" seem to stand mid-way between strong "objective" examples and "softer" or weaker ones. We may compare them with Austin's behabitives: I apologize, I bid you welcome, I am sorry, I approve, etc.[1] These are only situation-changing in a secondary way. (We shall note later that Evans sees them as factual presuppositions.) But one excellent way forward may appear by going back to Wittgenstein. When we mourn the death of a friend, he pointed out, we are not describing what we are doing, but *participating in an act of mourning*.[2] An apology, similarly, constitutes an act: an act *in* saying something. Thanksgiving, adoration, and praise in worship constitute liturgical *acts*.

Hence, it would not be accurate to deny that thanksgiving, adoration, or indeed blessing, are illocutionary acts (i.e., acts in the saying of them), to use Austin's term.[3] Searle is as enthusiastic

---

1. Austin, *How to Do Things with Words*, 83.
2. Wittgenstein, *Philosophical Investigations*, II.ix, 189.
3. Austin, *How to Do Things with Words*, 91, 98–131, 144–50.

as Austin about the term "illocution." Again, he writes, "It is only given such institutions as the church, the law, private property, the state, and the special position of the speaker and hearer within these institutions that one can excommunicate, appoint, give and bequeath one's possessions or declare war." He goes on to expand this: "When God says, 'Let there be light,' this is a declaration"[4] that is itself a creative act. Evans further expounds this point: a blessing, like a baptism, is not merely a statement but an illocution. That is why the Orthodox, Roman Catholics, and Anglicans restrict this role to ordained clergy. If a lay person in those churches were to say the blessing, it would not count as an illocution in Austin's sense of the word.

Patrick Miller devotes a special section of *They Cried to the Lord* to prayers of blessing.[5] He first describes the characteristic contexts of prayers of blessing in the Old Testament. These concern the family or tribe, especially when members of the family part or go forth on a journey. Isaac blesses Jacob when he sent him to Paddan Aram (Gen 28:1–4), and Naomi blesses her two daughters-in-law when she seeks to send them back to their mother's house (Ruth 1:8–9). As Jacob leaves home, Isaac prays, "May God give you of the dew of heaven, and of the fatness of the earth, and plenty of grain and wine" (Gen 27:28). Similarly when Rebecca was due to leave for her marriage, her brother and her mother pray, "May you, our sister, become thousands of myriads; may your offspring gain possession of the gates of their foes." In 2 Sam 7:29, David prays to God, "Now therefore may it please you to bless the house of your servant, so that it may continue forever before you; for you LORD God have spoken, and with your blessing shall the house of your servant be blessed for ever." The public worship of the community, Miller adds, may also be an occasion of blessing.

Miller recognizes the limitations of the outworn arguments about word magic, but nevertheless underlines the power of words in an illocutionary sense. He argues, "in the case of blessing, some

---

4. Searle, *Expression and Meaning*, 18.
5. Miller, *They Cried to the Lord*, 281–303.

instances seem to reflect a kind of power to shape the future in the very speaking of the words. Is it prayer or is it magic?" He rejects the supposedly easy answer of magic but develops what we mean by a prayer-wish form. He rightly argues that the power of these words of blessing comes from *God*, not primarily from a human speaker. Miller concludes:

> There is a kind of performative and declarative speech in which the speaking of the words brings something into effect. In contemporary life we experience this, for example, in such things as the declaration of marriage in a wedding ceremony. The declaration itself makes legal and real the marriage of the couple. In the Old Testament, the various Deuteronomic statements of the LORD, "I am hereby granting/giving you the land which I swore to your fathers to give you" are a kind of declarative or performative speech that hands the land over to the people and gives it a religio-legal claim upon the land. The notion of effective power blessing is not far from this kind of performative speech.[6]

Unfortunately Miller appears not to have drawn upon my 1974 article, "The Supposed Power of Words in the Biblical Writings" or he could have said much more about word magic and Austin's use of performative language. But we are in broad agreement. Many prayers of blessing are illocutions within the class of speech acts.

This suggests that we must think again if we are too ready to classify prayers of blessing as merely (to use Brümmer's phrase) "therapeutic meditation." A speech act changes situations. We have only to reflect how the giving and receiving of an apology may change a situation in public life. In Genesis Isaac exclaims, "I have blessed him—and blessed he shall be" (Gen 27:33). Then "Isaac trembled violently" and Esau "cried out with an exceedingly great and bitter cry" (27:34). No convention existed for the withdrawal of a blessing any more than a baptism can be recalled today. Searle writes, "Declarations are a very special category of speech acts" and

---

6. Miller, *They Cried to the Lord*, 287.

suggests a diagram "where *D* indicates the declarational illocutionary point; the direction of fit is both words-to-world and world-to-words because of the peculiar character of declarations."[7] They do not merely change situations; but they do not do less than this.

Donald Evans considers all five of Austin's category of performative utterances. He classifying thanking, praising, and apologizing, under the heading of behabitives.[8] He admits that in some cases "there is no obvious content to be abstracted. But," he adds, "there are factual presuppositions."[9] Normally thanksgiving, for example, would presuppose that God has enacted some blessing. Apology would imply a new direction of attitude, like repentance. In due course these may result in actions or change of actions. Evans writes that even if language is "behabitive," "this does not automatically eliminate the relevance of facts—factual presuppositions and sometimes factual content."[10] This may involve observable changes in situation, which may be described in cognitive terms. Nevertheless the biblical examples speak for themselves.

Miller includes among prayers of blessing the various blessings in Ruth, which he calls "Ruth: A Story of Blessing."[11] The very fact that these prayers of blessing are embedded in a narrative with a plot suggests that events that are in principle observable did occur. He begins with Naomi's blessing on her two daughters-in-law: "May the LORD deal kindly with you, as you have dealt with the dead and with me. LORD grant that you may find security, each of you in the house of your husband" (Ruth 1:8–9). Naomi commits the lives and futures of her two daughters-in-law to God. Nevertheless, in spite of the generality of the prayer for blessing, "The specificity of the prayer is implicit in the reference to 'the house of your husband.'"[12]

---

7. Searle, *Expression and Meaning*, 18–19.
8. Evans, *The Logic of Self-Involvement*, 34–36.
9. Evans, *The Logic of Self-Involvement*, 35.
10. Evans, *The Logic of Self-Involvement*, 35.
11. Miller, *They Cried to the Lord*, 290–93.
12. Miller, *They Cried to the Lord*, 291.

Prayers of Blessing

Miller's second example comes in Ruth 2:4, when Boaz encounters reapers in the field. They exchange greetings and he says to them, "The LORD be with you," and they answer "The LORD bless you." They are carrying on their normal daily lives, and exchange blessings in the midst of everyday life. The first encounter between Ruth and Boaz results also in blessing: "May the LORD reward you for your deeds, and may you have a full reward from the LORD, the God of Israel, under whose wings you have come for refuge" (Ruth 2:12). This is obviously more than a blessing, but hardly less than the blessing.

The fourth blessing occurs in Ruth 3:10 when Ruth daringly steals up to the sleeping Boaz, who responds, "May you be blessed by the LORD, my daughter; this last instance of your loyalty is better than the first: you have not gone after young men whether poor or rich."

Finally, when Ruth and Boaz are married and have a child, the women say to Naomi, "Blessed be the LORD, who has not left you this day without next of kin" (Ruth 4:14). Miller comments, "Here we encounter blessing as thanksgiving."[13] The empirical fact that emerges from the exchanges of blessings is, finally, the importance of Ruth's descendants.

Miller's final example of prayers of blessing is the Aaronic benediction, which he calls a paradigm of blessing. Numbers 6:22–27 recounts that the LORD spoke to Moses saying, "Speak to Aaron and his sons saying 'Thus shall you bless the Israelites: you shall say to them, 'The LORD bless you and keep you; the LORD make his face to shine upon you, and be gracious to you; the LORD lift up his countenance upon you, and give you peace.' So they shall put my name on the Israelites, and I will bless them.'" This blessing has had an influential history in both Judaism and Christian liturgy, where it stands as a model or paradigm of prayers of blessing. The blessing of the LORD, who is repeated as the subject, is invoked upon the community as a whole, and upon each individual that is part of it. Miller concludes, "in the Hebrew,

---

13. Miller, *They Cried to the Lord*, 292.

the subject of the final clause is emphatic: 'so shall they put my name on the Israelites, and *I* will bless them.'"[14]

This subject still requires further explanation. Our initial approach is partly influenced by Geoffrey Warnock's argument that performative utterance or speech acts may differ in strength or weakness.[15]

---

14. Miller, *They Cried to the Lord*, 296 (his italics).
15. Warnock, "Some Types of Performative Utterance."

8

Praise and Thanksgiving as Speech Acts

Prayers of blessing and joy: speech acts? Basic issues

THE WORD "BLESS" WHEN used of others ("the LORD bless you and keep you") concerns speaking God's goodness over them. However, when used of God ("Come, bless the LORD") it serves more as a mode of praise. It is this second aspect—prayers of joy and praise—that we examine in this chapter. We will consider the praise and joyous blessing of Hannah in 1 Sam 2 and Mary's parallel in Luke 1. But first, we need to consider whether acts of praise and blessing can be considered to be some form of speech act. For many it is debatable whether these may count as speech acts of prayer, but we shall argue otherwise.

Miller writes, "Praise is a public act."[1] Praise and blessing is associated, he says, with such acts as a solemn entry into the sanctuary, and a call to the people to "acknowledge" a given reality.[2] "Acknowledgement" seems to relate to what Evans calls

---

1. Miller, *The Cried to the Lord*, 207.
2. Miller, *The Cried to the Lord*, 208.

Part II: Prayer in the Biblical Writings

"an authoritative positive evaluation," even if this is "extremely complex."[3] Evans suggests that these border on being a mild form of a verdictive performative act and utterance. For praise suggests a positive verdict of the worshipper on all that God is and has done. As the saints say in Rev 15:3, "Great and amazing are your deeds, Lord God the Almighty! Just and true are your ways, King of the nations."

Miller similarly cites Ps 98:1–3: "O sing to the LORD a new song, for he has done marvelous things. His right hand and his holy arm have gotten him victory. The LORD has made known his victory; he has revealed his vindication in the sight of the nations. He has remembered his steadfast love and faithfulness to the house of Israel. All the ends of the earth have seen the victory of our God." The main point that Miller makes is that the acclamation of praise and blessing carries with it a clear *reason* for this positive evaluation.[4] Psalm 117:2 reflects this pattern: "Praise the LORD, all you nations! Extol him, all you peoples! For great is his steadfast love towards us, and the faithfulness of the LORD endures for ever. Praise the LORD!" Miller comments, "Its paradigmatic character for the community of faith rests not only on its content but also very much on the way it is a model of both the song of thanksgiving and the hymn of praise. It gives us, in effect, the 'shape' of praise."[5] Psalm 118:1–4 repeats the same form with a heaping up of praise, including seven imperatives in vv.1–4 to sing, rejoice, praise, bless, and so on. These turn the *call* to praise into the *act* of praise itself. Miller adds, "Such elaborated calls to praise also accent the notes of jubilation, joy, and singing. Invariably, the more extended imperative the more these notes are sounded."[6]

Clements selects a key feature of this kind of prayer that reflects a basic conviction: "God changes things!" and this fact is acknowledged as good.[7] Two closely parallel prayers of praise and

---

3. Evans, *The Logic of Self-Involvement*, 156.
4. Miller, *They Cried to the Lord*, 206.
5. Miller, *They Cried to the Lord*, 206.
6. Miller, *They Cried to the Lord*, 207.
7. Clements, *In Spirit and Truth*, 63.

Praise and Thanksgiving as Speech Acts

blessing, to which we referred above, are those of Hannah in 1 Sam 2:1–10 and the Song of Mary, the mother of Jesus, in Luke 1:46–55, otherwise known as the Magnificat. When she prays, Hannah has already received the gift of a child, who she bore to her husband, Elkanah. This prayer is not one of petition but one of praise, joy, and thanksgiving.

Hannah begins: "My heart exults in the LORD; my strength is exalted in my God. My mouth derides my enemies because I rejoice in my victory" (1 Sam 2:1; NRSV). Similarly Mary begins her prayer, "My soul magnifies the Lord, and my spirit rejoices in God my Savior, for he has looked with favor on the lowliness of his servant" (Luke 1:46–48; NRSV). Both women are from the poor and lowly, yet both stand at a point of crisis in history. Both stress that God may kill but he certainly brings to life; he may make poor, but he certainly makes rich; he may bring low but he certainly exalts. Clements comments, "What such a picture expresses is the assertion that our world, and all the forces which control it, are set under the guiding and controlling power of God."[8]

Clements explains that there was "a massive political and military threat facing the people, which they had neither the resources nor the moral fibre with which to cope. This crisis emanated from the Philistines, or Sea People, as the Egyptian records describe them."[9] They had already established themselves along the coastal strip of the land of Israel in the region that borders Egypt, with Gaza as one of their major cities. They were land-hungry and aggressive, with militarily well advanced and well-organized resources. On Israel's side the poor conduct of Eli's sons seriously diminished Israel's leadership. Yet Samuel would become a pivotal figure during this time of resistance and early kingship. Hence Clements sums up the key point of Hannah's prayer as "God changes things!" He adds, "Not only does the prayer affirm God's power to enrich and exalt but also God's ability to bring down, to abase, and to punish."[10] Hannah's prayer marks, for the biblical author, a

8. Clements, *In Spirit and Truth*, 63.
9. Clements, *In Spirit and Truth*, 60.
10. Clements, *In Spirit and Truth*, 64.

turning point in the story of Israel. From this point on providential remedy for Israel's spiritual and political ills is traced through the remarkable charismatic leadership provided by Samuel.

Mary's prayer in Luke 1:46–55 is probably based on a reading of Hannah's prayer. Although Mary was a country girl, and Galilee had a gentile reputation, she would have learned "the piety and liturgy of the synagogue. She was undoubtedly brought up in a very well-defined tradition with an almost rigidly defined role to play in it."[11] She was saturated in the Old Testament. On Mary's Song of Praise, Joseph Fitzmyer comments,

> It is good to recall the similarity of this Canticle with that of Hannah in 1 Sam. 2:1–10 in general. Both Mary and Hannah are women who praise God for the action that he has taken in choosing them to be mothers of instruments of his salvific intervention in Israel's history. The general pattern and purpose of the canticles are the same, and many of the details in the Magnificat echo those of the canticle of Hannah.[12]

But he also sees this song as pointing back to a number of further Old Testament passages, including Ps 69:31 ("I extol him") and Ps 103:17 ("his mercy is for those who fear him").

Mary's poetic parallelism is not due to Luke's imaginative artistry, but to Mary's phenomenal knowledge of the Old Testament and especially of the Psalms. Marshall, Fitzmyer, Green, and Nolland all emphasize points of contact between the Magnificat and the Psalms.[13] Green comments, "Luke has repeatedly characterized Mary as a person of low commercial status and now she speaks of her 'lowliness.'"[14] Hannah does the same. Green traces the same themes through Zechariah, Elizabeth, and Mary, in the tradition that has provided the impetus, framework, and imagery of this Song. It is a consequence, Green says, "solely of God's surprising

---

11. Clements, *In Spirit and Truth*, 209.
12. Fitzmyer, *The Gospel according to Luke 1–9*, 369.
13. Marshall, *The Gospel of Luke*, 82–85; Green, *The Gospel of Luke*, 97–104.
14. Green, *The Gospel of Luke*, 98.

Praise and Thanksgiving as Speech Acts

grace."[15] Clements concludes, "Mary was deeply affected by the much earlier prayer of Hannah at her rejoicing over the birth of Samuel."[16]

Undoubtedly Clements is right that these prayers *mark* changes in the world. But are they illocutionary speech acts? This may be doubted since they celebrate acts of God already promised; they do not initiate the changes *in* the saying of them. This may help us to define more clearly when prayers, like promises, constitute speech acts that change situations *in* the saying of them. We may recall that most examples that we have considered do constitute speech acts, even if not all of them.

Clements examines the song of Zechariah in Luke 1:67-79 (the Benedictus) among his many examples of biblical prayers of praise and blessing. Zechariah prays:

> Blessed be the Lord God of Israel, for he has looked favorably on his people and redeemed them. He has raised up a mighty savior for us in the house of his servant David, as he spoke through the mouth of his holy prophets from of old, that we would be saved from our enemies and from the hand of all who hate us. Thus he has shown the mercy promised to our ancestors, and has remembered his holy covenant, the oath that he swore to our ancestor Abraham, to grant us that we, being rescued from the hands of our enemies, might serve him without fear, in holiness and righteousness before him all our days. And you, child, will be called the prophet of the Most High; for you will go before the Lord to prepare his ways, to give knowledge of salvation to his people by the forgiveness of their sins. . . . To give light to those who sit in darkness and in the shadow of death, and to guide our feet into the way of peace.

Clements comments, "As a prayer of thanksgiving it puts into words the feeling of joy in all that God has made possible, and

---

15. Green, *The Gospel of Luke*, 103.
16. Clements, *In Spirit and in Truth*, 209.

Part II: Prayer in the Biblical Writings

especially for the coming of the kingdom of God, for which John the Baptist will serve as a Herald."[17]

So Zechariah's prayer is akin to the prayers of Hannah and Mary. On the other hand, might the Benedictus—unlike the prayers of the two women—function as a speech act? Perhaps *parts* of the prayer may function in the way. "And you, child, will be called the prophet of the Most High" might be a prediction, but it is probably more than this. Zechariah "was filled with the Holy Spirit" (v. 67). Hence, it is likely that this is a performative utterance on naming and possibly appointing for his task. The passage as recounted by Luke includes the performative utterance of naming in "He is to be called John" (v. 60). Zechariah's encounter with the angel Gabriel (Luke 1:8–23) not only establishes his priesthood; but also confirms the "change in situation" to which Clements alludes, when Zechariah is released from being dumb.

Miller takes as a further example of praise and blessing 1 Chr 16:34: "O give thanks to the LORD, for he is good; for his steadfast love endures forever."[18] This comes in the narrower context of the trees singing for joy because at the last judgement God will put all things right, and the wider context that the Ark is placed in the Tent. The Davidic psalm expresses thanks and praise to God. Allusions include the covenant (16:15–16). Acclamation is repeated in 16:40–41, where Heman and Jeduthun sing praises with trumpets and cymbals. 2 Chronicles 5:13 recounts, "It was the duty of the trumpeters and singers to make themselves heard in unison in praise and thanksgiving to the LORD . . . 'For he is good, and his steadfast love endures forever.'"[19] Ezra 3:10–11 described what the musicians were doing when they gave thanks and praised God. The solemn liturgical occasion marked more than mental recollection which could be expressed in propositions. It marked a "performance" in language and action.

Psalm 100 is familiar to many as the *Jubilate Deo*, which is sung in Anglican churches that use the Book of Common Prayer

---

17. Clements, *In Spirit and in Truth*, 221.
18. Miller, *They Cried to the Lord*, 205.
19. Miller, *They Cried to the Lord*, 205.

Praise and Thanksgiving as Speech Acts

in Morning Prayer Sunday by Sunday. It was part of the Gregorian Chant; Augustine refers to it; and it was specified to be sung at Lauds. The NRSV begins, "Make a joyful noise to the LORD, all the earth. Worship the LORD with gladness; come into his presence with singing. . . . Enter his gates with thanksgiving and his courts with praise. Give thanks to him and bless his holy name. For the LORD is good" (Ps 100:1, 3-5). It moves from a song of thanksgiving into examples of praise. Miller comments, "Its setting is the entrance into the sanctuary for worship."[20] Neil and Willoughby comment that it is "An appeal to all lands to sing God's praise . . . and an appeal to thank Him [God] publicly."[21] If we pursue the logic of Evans' argument (and perhaps also Searle's) this appeal in not "rhetorical" or merely causal, but constitutes a verdictive, commissive, or behabitive performative utterance in which "all nations" are invited to share.[22]

---

20. Miller, *They Cried to the Lord*, 207.
21. Neil and Willoughby, *The Tutorial Prayer Book*, 107.
22. Evans, *The Logic of Self-Involvement*, 71-78 and 80-93; Searle, *Expression and Meaning*, 14-29.

9

Requests

Prayers That Led to Changes in Situations

IN OUR INTRODUCTION TO Part II we compared Kant's view of prayer as wholly subjective, designed for the moral improvement of the one who is praying with the more traditional view of prayer as sometimes making a difference in our situation or in the world. Kant called this "churchly" prayer, but we called it biblical prayer, without setting aside the more "subjective" approach. Presumably prayers of petition tend sometimes to change situations, while confession, praise, and thanksgiving, are important indicators of self-involvement and moral improvement. We shall first consider sixteen examples of more traditional understandings of petitionary prayer in the Old Testament.

1. Prayers in Genesis

i. One of the earliest biblical examples of explicit prayer and answer is that of Hagar of her son in Gen 21:16. Hagar puts her child under a bush to die, lifts her voice in weeping, and cries out, "Do not let me look on the death of the child." Genesis narrates, "And God heard the voice of the boy; and the angel of the LORD called to Hagar from heaven and said to her, 'What troubles you Hagar? Do not be afraid; for God has heard the voice of the boy where he is. Come, lift up the boy and hold him fast with your hand, I will make a great nation of him.' Then God opened her eyes and she saw a well of water."

ii. An even more striking example occurs in the prayer of Eliezer, Abraham's servant, in Gen 24:12–14. He seeks God's help in securing a wife for Isaac, but with many specific details. He prays,

> Please grant me success today and show steadfast love to my master, Abraham. I am standing here by the spring of water, and the daughters of the townspeople are coming out to draw water. Let the girl to whom I shall say, "please offer your jar that I may drink," and who shall say, "Drink, and I will water your camels"—let her be the one whom you have appointed for your servant Isaac. By this I shall I know that you have shown steadfast love to my master.

This constitutes an almost bizarre example of specifying details with which Divine guidance is to be understood and followed. The narrative has an almost secular and modern ring to it. There is no question that the specific details of an observable situation are involved in the prayer and the answer to it.

iii. Still in the book of Genesis, Jacob prays a specific prayer in Gen 32:9–12. He prays, "Deliver me, please, from the hand of my brother, from the hand of Esau." He has addressed God as, "O God of my father Abraham and God of my father Isaac" and offers the motivation for God's response. Jacob prays: "I am not worthy of the least of all the steadfast love and all the faithfulness that you have shown to your servant, for with only my staff I crossed this Jordan and now I have become two companies." Patrick D. Miller helps us to identify the structure of many Old Testament prayers: address, motivation, petition, and response.[1]

---

1. Miller, *They Cried to the Lord*, 338–57.

Part II: Prayer in the Biblical Writings

2. Prayers in the Mosaic Era

iv. The intercession of Moses on behalf of the people brings a possible surprise in that it involves a "change of mind" on the part of God. In Exod 32:11-13 Moses addresses God with a complaint as well as a prayer:

> [Complaint] "O LORD, why does your wrath burn hot against your people whom you have brought out of the land of Egypt with great power and a mighty hand?
>
> [Motivation:] Why should the Egyptians say, 'It was with evil intent that he brought them out to kill them in the mountains and to consume them from the face of the earth?'
>
> [Petition] Turn from your fierce wrath, change your mind and do not bring disaster on your people. Remember Abraham, Isaac, and Israel your servants, how you swore to them by your own self saying, 'I will multiply your descendants like the stars of heaven and all this land I have promised I will give to your descendants, and they shall inherit it forever.'"
>
> [Response] And the LORD changed his mind about the disaster that he had planned to bring upon the people.

Miller's analysis of complaint, motivation, petition, and response brings out the force of this specific prayer.[2]

v. Moses provides a second example in Exod 32:31-32, although this petition does not provide complaint and motivation. It begins with confession, "Alas this people has sinned a great sin; they have made for themselves gods of gold." The petition is, "if you will only forgive their sin—but if not, blot me out of the book." The narrative continues to show God's mercy and forbearance. It may, however, be accounted as a prayer that brings an observable result in Israel's situation. Moses has shown himself to be a true mediator. Ryder Smith comments that Moses was like a man torn in two, both one with God and one with the people.[3] Genuine

---

2. Miller, *They Cried to the Lord*, 339-40.
3. Smith, *The Bible Doctrine of Salvation*, 26-29 and 100-102.

intercessory prayer requires a mediator who wholly sympathizes with each of the two sides.

vi. A further example of specific prayer comes in Num 12:13, where Moses prays to God to heal Miriam's leprosy. He prays, "O God, please heal her," but the response is ambiguous. Miriam remains outside the camp, but when she is brought in, the march continues. Ambiguous answers remind us of the difference between brute persuasion (i.e., the causal or rhetorical force of Austin's perlocutions) and the institutional or performative force of Austin's illocutions. These have an effect *in* saying something; they do not have an effect *by* saying something.[4] Austin states, "The illocutionary act . . . may involve conventions. . . . By doing *x*, I was doing *y*."[5] In biblical thought the "conventions" are covenant promises. Prayer anticipates or expects answers and changes in situations but is never an attempt "to twist God's arm." This constitutes one reason why Paul dissociates the power of the word in 1 Cor 1:18–25 from the power of rhetoric.[6]

vii. In Num 27:16–17 Moses asks the LORD to appoint a leader, since he is forbidden to enter the promised land. His petition is: "Appoint someone over the congregation who shall go out before them and come in before them, who shall lead them out and bring them in." The response is that the LORD tells Moses to take Joshua and commission him as leader. Here clearly is an example of prayer that has objective and observable consequences.

3. Prayers in the period of the Judges

viii. In the period of the Judges Gideon perceived that the angel of the LORD had met him, and prayed "Help me, LORD God. For I have seen the angel of the LORD face-to-face." In response "the LORD said to him, 'Peace be to you; do not fear, you shall not die'" (Judg 6:22). Similarly Manoah entreats the LORD for help

---

4. Austin, *How to Do Things with Words*, 101–31.
5. Austin, *How to Do Things with Words*, 106.
6. Brown, *The Cross and Human Transformation*, 13–63.

and what he should do with Samson in Judg 13:8–9. He prays, "O LORD I pray, let the man of God whom you sent come to us again and teach us what we are to do concerning the boy who will be born." God's response was, "God listened to Minoah, and the angel of God came again to the woman as she sat in the field" (v. 9).

ix. In Judg 16:28 Samson, who has been blinded, prays for strength to pull down pillars of the temple of Dagon. He prays, "LORD God, . . . remember me and strengthen me only this once, so that with this one act of revenge I may pay back the Philistines for my two eyes." No *explicit* response is recorded, but Samson grasped the pillars and pulls the temple down.

4. Prayers in Kings and Chronicles

x. In 1 Kgs 3:6–12 and 2 Chr 1:8–10 God appears to Solomon with the promise, "Ask what I should give you." Solomon prays, "Give your servant therefore an understanding mind to govern your people, able to discern between good and evil, for who can govern this great people?" The response is: "It pleased the LORD that Solomon had asked this. God said to him . . . 'I now do according to your word. Indeed, I give you a wise and discerning mind.'" In spite of Solomon's follies, the kingdom achieved its greatest extent under his reign, together with huge economic prosperity. The accounts of his subsequent arbitration between two prostitutes acquired legendary status (1 Kgs 3:16–28).

xi. Elijah furnishes us with several relevant examples, not least in 1 Kgs 17:17–24. The son of the widow with whom Elijah lived comes near death and she accuses him of having brought about the illness. Elijah takes the child to his bed and laid him down. He then cries out, "O LORD my God, have you brought calamity even upon the widow with whom I am staying by killing her son?" He then stretched himself upon the child three times and cried out to the LORD a second time: "O LORD my God, have you brought calamity even upon the widow?" He then prays a second prayer: "O LORD my God, let this child's life come into him again." The response is: "The LORD listened to the voice of Elijah; the life of the child came into him again and he revived." This is clearly an example of an answer to prayer that was observable and could in principle be empirically verified.

xii. A still more famous example occurs in 1 Kgs 18:36–37. Elijah prays for God to rain down fire on his offering in the contest with the prophets of Ba'al on Mount Carmel. He prays, "O LORD, God of Abraham, Isaac, and Israel, . . . let it be known this day that you are God in Israel, that I am your servant, and that I have done all these things at your bidding. Answer me, O LORD, answer me, so that this people may know that you, O LORD, are God, and that you have turned their hearts back." The divine response is that the fire of the LORD fell and consumed the burnt offering. The people fell on their faces and said, "The LORD indeed is God; the LORD indeed is God."[7]

xiii. Whatever some may claim about the historicity of the Elisha narratives in 2 Kgs 3–13, the narrator boldly recounts Elijah's prayer for illumination for his servant in the face of the Aramean army. Elisha prays, "O LORD, please open his eyes that he may see." The response is: "So the LORD opened the eyes of the servant and he saw" (2 Kgs 6:17).

xiv. A further striking example of prayer and response that can be empirically verified in principle concerns the prayers of Hezekiah in 2 Kgs 19:14–19, with parallels in Isa 37:14–20 and 2 Chr 32:20. Hezekiah prayed to the LORD on receiving the message of Sennacherib, the King of Assyria, challenging the power of the God of Israel to keep Jerusalem from being handed over to the Assyrian King. Hezekiah prays, "Incline your ear, O LORD, and hear; open your eyes, O LORD, and see; hear the words of Sennacherib. . . . So now, O LORD our God, save us I pray you, from his hand so that all the kingdoms of the earth may know that you, O LORD, are God alone." The divine response is, "Thus says the LORD God of Israel: I have heard your prayer to me about King Sennacherib of Assyria. . . . He shall not come in this city or shoot an arrow there, come before it with a shield, or cast a siege-ramp against it" (vv. 20, 32).

---

7. Miller, *They Cried to the Lord*, 350–51.

Part II: Prayer in the Biblical Writings

xv. Finally before the exile we may allude to Hezekiah's prayer when he became sick to the point of death. 2 Kings 20:3, with a parallel in Isa 38:3, recounts: "Hezekiah became sick and was at the point of death.... Hezekiah wept bitterly." He prayed, "LORD I implore you, remember now how I have walked before you in faithfulness with a whole heart and have done what is good in your sight." The divine response is: "Thus says the LORD, the God of your ancestor David: I have heard your prayer, I have seen your tears; indeed I will heal you; on the third day you shall go up to the house of the LORD. I will add fifteen years to your life. I will deliver you and this city out of the hand of the king of Assyria; I will defend the city for my own sake and for my servant David's sake." This prayer and its response reflect an objective and in principle observable situation.

xvi. 2 Chronicles 14:11 continues this royal narrative with reference to King Asa, who faces Zerah the Ethiopian in battle. He cries to the LORD, "Help us, O LORD our God, for we rely on you, and in your name we have come against this multitude. LORD, you are our God, let no mortal prevail against you." The Divine response is: "So the LORD defeated the Ethiopians before Asa, and before Judah, and the Ethiopians fled" (v. 18). To these sixteen clear examples we could add others, such as the prayers of Jeremiah and Nehemiah, but enough has been said to establish the clear patterns of petition in Scripture.

Are such requests speech acts? Yes, for the uttering of such a prayer constitutes *a request* to God that he act. Request, of course, is a very different kind of speech act from a command. The one requesting cannot *demand* that God act nor can they *guarantee* a positive response from God. As such, both humility and hope are part of the proper posture in intercession. But requests within the context of certain kinds of relationship are entirely appropriate and the one of whom the request is made might well be expected to answer. In the case of Israel, the basis of that relationship is the covenant itself—God's faithful commitment to his people. And God would be expected to be faithful to that covenant. While worshippers cannot presume to know precisely what that means in specific circumstances, they do believe that it forms a basis for trusting in God's loving disposition towards his people, and his desire that they flourish. And it is with this belief that requests are made in faith and expectation.

And such requests are believed to have an effect. Things happen as God responds to the prayers of his people that would not otherwise have happened. In this way, prayer is believed, albeit indirectly, to effect real change in the world. How so? By affecting the God who acts in response to requests. Intercession and petition are thus a paradigm case of the place of prayer in the interpersonal relationship between God and his people.

Concluding Summary

PROMISE IS A FUNDAMENTAL category in the communication from God to humankind. In the past, the biblical writers, William Tyndale, and Martin Luther argued for this or implied it, and in contemporary thought Wolfhart Pannenberg and Jürgen Moltmann similarly underlined its centrality. It is astonishing and remarkable that Almighty God is willing to bind himself by a commissive act of promise that limits his action to those consistent with the promises.

Promise and prayer are deeply inter-personal acts or transactions between God and his people. They represent what Martin Buber called an I-Thou relation between God and his people. True prayer, according to Paul, is a Divine dialogue prompted and initiated by God the Holy Spirit. It is not initiated by humankind. Thus, God is not simple the one who responds to prayer but also the one who inspires prayer.

And what of speech-act theory? Austin first argued that a performative utterance would count as an act provided that it functioned in the context of an institutional fact. To appoint or to authorize someone constitutes a clear example. A speech act such as appointing requires a social institution, like government or church, with its rules and authorized roles. Appointing someone to a role within that framework can only be done by an already-authorized person or people in circumstances governed by the rules, and with the right words. In other words, the appointing

Concluding Summary

speech only counts as appointing, as doing something, if done by the right person in the right context with the right words.

Promising is certainly a classic example of performative language: when someone promises to do something they are, by the very uttering of the promise, acting, making a commitment to a future course of action. The words change the situation. In addition to this, promise is a *commissive* performative, as Austin and Searle confirm. Speech acts based on institutions are *self-involving*, as Evans and others argue. This enables us to distinguish institutional force from merely causal force, and therefore illocutions from perlocutions. It also enables us to escape from outdated and fallacious arguments about word-magic.

We examined promise in the Old and New Testaments. God's promise to Abraham was foundational, promising land and descendants. It was renewed to Moses, Joshua, and through Nathan to David and Solomon. Promises, however, need not always be explicit; sometimes a verbal future indicative (such as "I'll be there") may function as a promise. Whether God's promise may be conditional is debated: do Old Testament promises depend on Israel's obedience? Many certainly do, but arguably the underpinning covenant relationship itself, which was unconditionally initiated by God with Abraham and was sustained by God in the face of persistent disobedience by Israel, depends on God's fidelity alone (cf. Rom 11).

In the New Testament, "promise" is prominent especially in Paul and Hebrews, although also present in Acts. Paul uses the concept repeatedly in Rom 4:3, 13–14, and Gal 3:7, and the writer to Hebrews in Heb 4:1 and chapter 6. The New Testament emphasizes the fulfilment of God's promises to Israel, but alongside that it still speaks of what still remains to be fulfilled. Both aspects—the now and the not-yet—relate to the work of the Holy Spirit, who is poured out according to promise, but of whom there is much more to come.

We have tried to address the problem of God's promises in the biblical writings that are addressed to specific people but may be appropriated today indiscriminately. We need to avoid two extremes. One extreme may be the claim that all God's promises are universally applicable, even if some pertain to particular situations or people. But the opposite extreme would be to approach all promises with skepticism, as being so tied in with the particular situations in which they were given that they cannot have wider applicability. Some of God's promises, we argued, are indeed timeless, universal, and unconditional. Many are addressed to the whole people of God. So a sane and rational approach, a middle way between the extremes, would be to take account of to whom each promise is addressed and what conditions and limitations are placed on it by its originating context.

In our second part on prayer, we acknowledged that a purely "subjective" account of prayer could hardly lead to the notion or prayer as a speech act. And some prayer, such as meditative prayer, is certainly not a form of speech act. But where prayer is understood as genuine communication between people and God, possibilities emerge.

Granted, prayer does not *automatically* change situations; indeed, not all prayer even *seeks* to change situations. Nevertheless, some prayer has the form of requests and that usually does seek a change in the world. And if such requests are answered by God, as they sometimes are in Scripture, then the prayer really made a difference. Thus, promise is always a speech act if it is sincere; and prayer *may* be a speech act, depending on the kind of prayer it is.

Prayer would admittedly not be a speech act if we were to adopt Kant's notion of "rational" prayer, which Brümmer calls therapeutic meditation, i.e. it is a merely subjective exercise. However, we have seen that in Scripture prayer is often speech aimed at changing the world, albeit indirectly, by invoking Divine help. And there is no question that this is how the Christian tradition has understood prayer. Our many biblical examples demonstrated that when God chooses to answer prayer, prayer can lead to changes of situation or reality. In Genesis some of the lesser-known prayers plead for "objective" states of affairs to take place. Eliezer prayed for particular circumstances in his prayer concerning his search for a bride for Isaac; Hagar's prayer lead to changes in Ishmael's

Concluding Summary

situation (Gen 21:16); Moses prayed for Miriam's healing. In the New Testament examples abound.

As we have said before there are many kinds of prayer in the Bible. Clements points out that the four main types are petitionary prayer or asking for things; intercession or praying on behalf of others; confession or contrition; and praise and thanksgiving. A study of Hebrew and Greek terms confirms this. Examples of all four types are found in the Pentateuch, Kings and Chronicles, Psalms, and the New Testament. These correspond respectively to different types of speech acts. To Clements' list we noted other kinds of prayer, such as blessing and lament.

So what kind of speech acts are prayer? Well, that depends on the kind of prayer under discussion. Consider confession, thanksgiving, and praise. Perhaps the nearest parallel to these is what Austin called "behabitives." He listed in this category such terms as "apologizing," which might be akin to confession of failure or rebellion; and "thanking," which is very like thanksgiving in worship. Here the one praying is adopting a certain attitude by means of their praying as they do. This is a form of speech act, albeit a weak form.

Prayers of blessing probably represent a special category of performative utterances. Isaac, Jacob, Ruth, Boaz, and Naomi, all offer or receive blessings. Miller calls these "a kind of performative," comparable to a declarative pronouncement at a wedding. Searle calls them, "a special category of speech act" in which the direction of fit is both word-to-world and world-to-word. The priestly or Aaronic blessing in Num 6:22–27 represents an example.

Then we have petitions and intercessions—requests. As *request*, intercessory and petitionary prayer is a very different kind of speech act to promising. Those making promises are committing themselves (or the community they are authorized to represent) to certain courses of action. (Promises made on behalf of those we are not authorized to represent do not count as promises and are not effective as speech acts.) But those making requests are calling upon *someone else* to act in a situation. As such, the one making a request cannot bring about the granting of the request simply by the act of making it. To one degree or another, the response is in the gift of the one addressed. Nevertheless, in making a request the one doing so is still performing a speech act, the act of inviting a response from another. And, as we saw, things can be granted in response to requests that may not otherwise have been given: "You do not have because you do not ask God," as James says (Jas 4:2).

Furthermore, certain institutional facts may affect the likelihood of a request being granted. For instance, as Jesus said, if one asks one's father for bread one has good grounds for expecting bread, not a stone (Matt 7:9). The nature of the child-parent relationship itself has implications for how requests are handled. In the case of prayer, the underpinning institution is God's covenant relationship with his people. That is the basis upon which God is petitioned. And as we have seen in this book, many requests are for God to act in accordance with his covenant promises. This affects the level of expectation that those praying may have and also the depths of lament experienced when God *seems* to be abandoning his people (e.g., Ps 44).

Searle, Evans, and others have shown the importance of institutional facts to speech acts. Promise is a speech act because it rests on an institution. In the case of God's promises in Scripture, that institution is the covenant. We have seen that this very same covenant is also the institution underpinning prayer in the biblical tradition, making promise and prayer aspects of God's interpersonal, covenant relationship with his people.

Appendix

Developments in Speech-Act Theory and Biblical Studies

IN THIS APPENDIX WE seek to sketch the insights from different speech-act theorists in relation to biblical studies.

1. Evans, Recanati, and Wolterstorff: Onlooks, "Counting As," and Institutions

Donald Evans

Donald D. Evans (1927–2018) was a Canadian educator, who gained an Oxford D.Phil. and was Professor of Divinity at McGill. He points out that to understand thanksgiving and blessing as speech acts entails regarding them as acts of "*acknowledgement*."[1] He writes, "The word 'acknowledge' has a performative aspect.... I imply that I have certain intentions or attitudes, and I commit myself to certain behaviour."[2] He adds, "If I actually acknowledge how much you have done for me, I not only say something to you, I also think and act accordingly."[3] This is bound up with

---

1. Evans, *The Logic of Self-Involvement*, 41–43; cf. 66–78 and 79–95.
2. Evans, *The Logic of Self-Involvement*, 42
3. Evans, *The Logic of Self-Involvement*, 42.

Appendix

the speaker and addressee having certain institutional roles and status.[4]

In Evans' language the institution or covenant constitutes a "system" in which "onlooks" appear.[5] "Onlooks" constitute one of the most important and distinctive features of Donald Evans' book, *The Logic of Self-Involvement*. Yet out of a book of nearly 300 pages he spends barely ten pages expounding the concept apart from scattered allusions.[6] He stresses that the concept is not individualistic but owes much to Wittgenstein's notion of "seeing as."[7] Wittgenstein used the example of the duck-rabbit, in which an object could be seen now as a duck and now as a rabbit.[8] Looking on something as something else involves seeing it within a system or structure and ascribing a status to it.[9]

I have applied this conception of "onlooks" to justification by grace through faith alone in *The Two Horizons* and elsewhere.[10] Within the framework or system of law, I argue, humankind is seen by God as sinful. But within the framework or system of eschatology and faith humanity is seen as righteous. This is no mere paradox or legal fiction. Two *propositions* may relate to each other as contradictions, but not two *evaluations* from within *different systems* (in this case, law and eschatology). Strictly, humankind's sin is a matter of brute fact; humankind's righteousness is an institutional fact, based on grace and the covenant. God sees redeemed human beings as righteous "in Christ" through faith. In this light, we can see the truth of Evans' claim that onlooks are practical and serious.

    4. Evans, *The Logic of Self-Involvement*, 66–78
    5. Evans, *The Logic of Self-Involvement*, 124–41.
    6. Evans, *The Logic of Self-Involvement*, 137–41.
    7. Wittgenstein, *Philosophical Investigations*, sects. 74, 228, and II, 193–208.
    8. We might also compare with Nicholas Wolterstorff analogous idea of "counting as" (x counts as y) in *Divine Discourse*, a work postdating that of Evans.
    9. Evans, *The Logic of Self-Involvement*, 127.
    10. This argument is worked out in detail in *The Two Horizons* and in an article for the Berlin Academy. Thiselton, *The Two Horizons*, 415–31; and Thiselton, "On the Logical Grammar of Justification in Paul."

John Ziesler writes, "If God looks on believers only as they are found in Christ, he may properly declare them righteous, for in him . . . they are righteous. . . . There is nothing fictional here."[11] In Wittgenstein's terminology each verdict appears within the context of a distinct language game.[12]

François Recanati

The work of François Recanati (b. 1952) is also important for speech-act theory. He has taught at Harvard and the University of California and is a Research Fellow at the Centre National de la Recherche Scientifique in Paris. One of his main books is *Meaning and Force* (1987). Following the work of William Alston, Recanati explores the idea of "potential illocutions." Recanati is interested in *context*, and urges the importance for speech-act theory concerning what the hearer infers and what the speaker intends in understanding whether an utterance counts as a speech act.[13] In the absence of definitive knowledge of both, the utterance is a "projection" of its illocutionary force.

Recanati relates speech-act theory to semantics and continues to distinguish between content and force. A more recent book is *Perspectival Thought: A Plea for (Moderate) Relativism*.[14] This expounds his "contextualism," i.e., the theme that every kind of meaning and force depends on its specific context. His interest in conversation and implicature brings him at times close to H. P. Grice.

---

11. Ziesler, *The Meaning of Righteousness in Paul*, 16a.

12. Wittgenstein, *Philosophical Investigations*, sect. 74 and II. xi, 193–214; and Wittgenstein, *Zettel*, sects. 195–235.

13. Recanati, *Meaning and Force*, 36–39.

14. Recanati, *Perspectival Thought*.

Appendix

Nicholas Wolterstorff

Nicholas Wolterstorff (b.1932) was educated at Calvin College, Grand Rapids, and Harvard, and is now Emeritus Noah Porter Professor of Philosophy at Yale University. He has written prodigiously on epistemology, philosophy of religion, and political philosophy. He is associated with Alvin Plantinga and William Alston and is an advocate of Reformed Epistemology. In *Divine Discourse* he discusses what he calls "count-generation," in which the words of human writers can "count as" the voice of God. He subtitles this book: *Philosophical Reflections on the Claim That God Speaks*.

Wolterstorff gives some illuminating example of "count generation." He begins with Augustine's experience of hearing the voices of children "as" the voice of God.[15] This leads to a discussion of "speech-action theory" and "illocutionary actions."[16] Promising at once appears as a good example of speech acts. This is because the speaking of a promise (given the conditions of sincerity, etc.) constitutes the very act of commitment.[17] Propositional content is distinguished from illocutionary force.[18] For example, in the sentence, "I promise that I will come" "I will come" represents the propositional content; and "I promise that" represents the illocutionary or performative force. Speech-action, he says, can function as illocutionary action.[19] He cites for example a person's extending his arm out of a car window to signal that he intends to turn.[20] Wolterstorff uses this example because sticking one's arm out of a car window *counts as* an act of promising to turn left or right.[21]

In his discussion of "double agency discourse" he opens the way for "deputized discourse." A secretary, for example, can type

---

15. Wolterstorff, *Divine Discourse*, 5–8.
16. Wolterstorff, *Divine Discourse*, 11 and 19.
17. Cf. Thiselton, "The Paradigm of Biblical Promise as Trustworthy, Temporal, Transformative Speech-Action."
18. Wolterstorff, *Divine Discourse*, 20.
19. Wolterstorff, *Divine Discourse*, 37.
20. Wolterstorff, *Divine Discourse*, 78–79.
21. Wolterstorff, *Divine Discourse*, 83–89.

Developments in Speech-Act Theory and Biblical Studies

a letter that is really from the director. The crucial thing is for the secretary to know the mind of the director. A second example would be the ambassador who speaks on behalf of the head of state. Wolterstorff writes, "The head of state performs illocutionary acts by way of the ambassador performing illocutionary acts."[22] Thus, God speaks through the prophets, who speak a deputized discourse.

In the example of the signal concerning the car, the *causal* force of the turn is his hand turning the steering wheel; the *institutional* force of the turn is the hand signal. The effect of the institutional cause depends on other drivers' recognizing the signal as *counting as* what it indicates.[23] When God speaks through a deputy there is an understanding of the conventions and institutions which make deputized discourse possible.

Wolterstorff points out that here one action (extending one's hand) can count as another (indicating a turn). He adds another simile for how speech acts work: the rules of chess. The moves in chess are *institutional* and determine what is to *count as* "check mate" or winning the game. The driver and chess-player "do really perform a speech act."[24] (These actions are genuinely speech-acts because they count as [i.e., function in place of] acts of speech. Of course this depends on convention or on socially-established practices or traditions.) Wolterstorff appeals to Searle and then to Alvin Goldman for the dictum: "Only if there is a convention in effect, or something convention-like, will A count as B."[25] As Searle (and Briggs, as we shall see) rightly insist these must be constitutive rules which in turn depend on institutions. As we have argued, in the biblical writings the pre-eminent "institution" or "convention-like" institution is the covenant.

Wolterstorff compares simply "winning" a game, which he calls a brute fact, with observing the rules of the game, which he regards as an "institutional" fact and which makes winning the

22. Wolterstorff, *Divine Discourse*, 45.
23. Wolterstorff, *Divine Discourse*, 80–81.
24. Wolterstorff, *Divine Discourse*, 79.
25. Goldman, *A Theory of Human Action*, 25–26.

game possible. He observes, "The entire system of rules . . . provide one with ways of winning."[26] The "institution" tells us what "counts as" winning.[27] In physical terms two children may look alike, but one has a special standing as, for example, crown prince; in the system of law or morality "It seems no great mystery that a child . . . [is] crown prince."[28] Once again, Wolterstorff argues that only an umpire can pronounce someone "Out!"; yet in this context the player *really is* out. Changes in institutional facts can lead to genuine changes in brute facts or to situations in the world.

Wolterstorff further discusses whether God might have the rights and duties of one who speaks. He writes, "It is inherent in making a promise or covenant that one obligates oneself to do something."[29] He adds, "The implication that God cannot make promises or covenants should, in my judgment, be unsettling."[30] Here he is entering dialogue with William Alston. He regards Alston as being indebted here to Kant, for the view that a holy will has no obligations. But why agree with Kant? After all, any Divine obligations are not imposed on God from outside but are *self-imposed*. Furthermore, "Certain actions are character-required of God."[31] God acts in character as a loving person. God's acting through human writers in the Bible depends on institutional causes and processes. This study is most illuminating for biblical interpreters.

In a 2001 essay, Wolterstorff reapplies and extends some of his material on deputized discourse or "double-agency discourse."[32] He writes, "Paradigmatic cases are those in which one person has been deputized to speak in behalf of another, so that the latter performs an illocutionary act by way of the former performing some

26. Wolterstorff, *Divine Discourse*, 81.
27. Wolterstorff, *Divine Discourse*, 82.
28. Wolterstorff, *Divine Discourse*, 85.
29. Wolterstorff, *Divine Discourse*, 100.
30. Wolterstorff, *Divine Discourse*, 101.
31. Wolterstorff, *Divine Discourse*, 111.
32. Wolterstorff, "The Promise of Speech-Act Theory for Biblical Interpretation," 83.

Developments in Speech-Act Theory and Biblical Studies

locutionary act (and perhaps some illocutionary act as well)."[33] Double-agency discourse, he says, enables us to understand Scripture as the manifestation of God speaking by way of human beings speaking. God performs illocutionary acts by way of human beings having performed locutionary and illocutionary acts.

This way of understanding Scripture provides "a way of breaking out of the sterile impasse among defenders of authorial-discourse interpretation and performance interpretation."[34] In the earlier part of his essay, Wolterstorff traced the attractiveness and limitations of these approaches represented respectively by Schleiermacher and Gadamer.[35] He reiterates, "God speaks by way of Scripture."[36] We need not worry, he argues, if this is through sixty-six different books. The canon of Scripture provides something like Schleiermacher's hermeneutical circle whereby we interpret the parts in the light of the whole, and the whole in the light of the parts.[37] This sophisticated approach to hermeneutics is based on speech-act theory and vindicates it.

The essays by Kevin Vanhoozer and Dan Stiver in the same volume also contribute to speech-act theory in their own way.[38] Vanhoozer discusses relevance theory and the co-operative principle of H. Paul Grice under the general notion of communicative action in communication. Like Searle and Wolterstorff he considers promise as "the paradigmatic speech act."[39] He then rightly underlines the importance of the covenant in this context, as we have

---

33. Wolterstorff, "The Promise of Speech-Act Theory for Biblical Interpretation," 83.

34. Wolterstorff, "The Promise of Speech-Act Theory for Biblical Interpretation," 83.

35. Wolterstorff, "The Promise of Speech-Act Theory for Biblical Interpretation," 73–82.

36. Wolterstorff, "The Promise of Speech-Act Theory for Biblical Interpretation," 84.

37. Wolterstorff, "The Promise of Speech-Act Theory for Biblical Interpretation," 86.

38. *After Pentecost* (2001), edited by Craig Bartholomew et al.

39. Vanhoozer, "From Speech Acts to Scripture Acts," 16.

also argued. Like Wolterstorff he sees God's speaking as manifested through illocutionary speech acts based on the covenant.[40]

Dan Stiver covers similar ground, examining in particular the relationship between history and fiction. He is not content with Hans Frei's notion of "history-likeness" as a concept which can be applied to the Gospel narratives. Perhaps surprisingly he brings together Paul Ricoeur and J. L. Austin to provide a larger conceptual framework than Hans Frei offers. Speech acts, he believes, help towards an integration of history and fiction.[41]

2. Briggs and Neufeld or White and Botha? Speech Acts, Biblical Interpretation, and Constatives.

Richard S. Briggs is Director of Biblical Studies in St. John's College, University of Durham and author of *Words in Action*, and several research articles on speech-act theory.[42] He relates together and compares the work of Evans, Searle, and Wolterstorff in his discussion of the contrast between institutional facts and brute facts.[43] All three writers use the notion of one utterance or action "counting as" another. Briggs calls these "constitutive" rules, which "create the possibility of new forms of behaviour by saying that a certain activity X will . . . count as activity Y in context C."[44] All three stress the pivotal importance of institutional facts (in contrast to brute facts, as Anscombe calls them) for example in acquiring a status in marriage or in most games.

In these works the bridegroom's "I do" and an umpire's "out!" shape reality through an institutional performative utterance. Rights and responsibilities relate closely to *institutional* facts. In this kind of language, Searle argues (as we have seen), "We impose

---

40. Vanhoozer, "From Speech Acts to Scripture Acts," 38-44.

41. Stiver, "Ricoeur, Speech-act Theory, and the Gospels in History," 62-69.

42. Briggs, *Words in Action*; Briggs, "Speech-Act Theory"; Briggs, *Reading the Bible Wisely*, 58-72 and 147-82.

43. Briggs, *Words in Action*, 58-60, 211-14, 228-31.

44. Briggs, *Words in Action*, 58; Searle, *Speech Acts*, 33-35; Wolterstorff, *Divine Discourse*, 75-94, especially 78-84.

rights, responsibilities, obligations, duties, privileges."[45] All these things are relevant to different kinds of promise and prayer in the biblical writings.

It will have become apparent that our consideration of developments in speech-act theory does not occur in chronological sequence. Developments interact and crisscross in ways that make chronological ordering difficult, if not impossible. Further, the relations of these developments specifically to biblical studies also varies. Austin and Grice did not explore the issue at all; Searle's mention of religion was marginal at most, considering the church as a useful example of relevant institutions; Evans, however, aims to integrate the two disciplines fully, and he is followed in this respect by Wolterstorff, Briggs, White, Neufeld, and Botha. These last two focus on a particular stretch of biblical language (1 John and John 4), while White devotes an entire number of *Semeia* to considering speech acts and biblical studies as an entire discipline.

Briggs was one of my best PhD graduates at Nottingham, and he has produced a comprehensive account of the relation between speech-act theory and biblical interpretation. Briggs begins by declaring, "Speech-act theory provides tools for analysing uses of language, in particular uses which are strongly self-involving."[46]

Jennifer Hornsby also argues (in 1994) that certain social conditions must apply for a speech act to be successful.[47] Briggs supports this conclusion. The reason why this present discussion does not contradict our earlier "preliminary approach" concerning "weaker" speech acts is because, in Briggs' words, "A performative utterance is a certain kind of 'multiple' illocutionary act, and explicit performatives are not the same special case in Austin's original thinking as strong illocutions."[48] There are more than one kind of illocutionary act. Sometimes we must resist a generalizing answer about speech acts. Biblical examples of promises and prayer may require careful exegesis before their philosophical and

45. Searle, *The Construction of Social Reality*, 100.
46. Briggs, *Words in Action*, 17.
47. Hornsby, "Illocution and its Significance" 198; cf. 187–207.
48. Briggs, *Words in Action*, 68.

Appendix

linguistic status emerges. He agrees with Neufeld that speech-act theory entails "reconceiving exegesis itself."[49] Briggs builds on Neufeld's work admirably. This includes from the text of 1 John "boasts, denials, and confessions" as Duane Watson expresses it.[50] In addition to my own work, Briggs considers the contribution of Vanhoozer and others.[51]

Chapter 2 of Briggs' *Words in Action* examines speech-act theory as a linguistic phenomenon. He traces the work of Austin, so-called Oxford philosophy, and a background in Wittgenstein. This leads on to a study of Searle, whose series of books Briggs calls, "by far the most comprehensive account of speech act theory."[52] He traces Searle's modification of Austin's taxonomy of illocutionary acts and discusses the role of intentionality. He provides a helpful discussion of institutional facts and background.[53] He then considers the work of H. P. Grice and Recanati.

In chapter 3 Briggs considers texts in the light of Derrida's challenge. As Werner Jeanrond asserts, text as communication presupposes an agent of communication, even if literary theorists repeatedly emphasize the role of readers.[54] Typically Derrida insisted that written texts "subsist" beyond their moment of inscription; they are "ruptured" from their originating context.[55] Derrida also takes exception to Austin's work on the relation between performatives and constatives. He pleads for "total context," which includes the conscious presence of speakers and much else. Allegedly Austin ends up in "a paradoxical but unavoidable confusion."[56] In place of this, Derrida suggests "iterability" to

---

49. Briggs, *Words in Action*, 18.

50. Watson, "Rhetorical Criticism of Hebrews and the Catholic Epistles since 1978."

51. Vanhoozer, "The Semantics of Biblical Literature"; and Vanhoozer, *Is There a Meaning in this Text?*

52. Briggs, *Words in Action*, 43.

53. Briggs, *Words in Action*, 58–63.

54. Jeanrond, *Text and Interpretation*, 73–75; Briggs, *Words in Action*, 75.

55. Derrida, *Limited Inc.*

56. Derrida, *Limited Inc.*, 17

make possible successful performative.⁵⁷ For example, signatures are effective because they are iterable or repeatable.

Briggs considers Searle's reply to Derrida. This is problematic because Searle distances himself from both Austin and Derrida.⁵⁸ Nevertheless Searle's work on the logic of illocutionary acts remains clear and helpful. The difficulties that Derrida faces also confront the radical Reader Response theory of the later Stanley Fish. On the other hand, Briggs discusses the example of Coriolanus' appointment to office as an illocutionary act. Of Coriolanus "He says, it is *about* what the theory is 'about.'"⁵⁹ In his article on speech-act theory, Briggs cites Stanley Fish as saying, "The constative use turns out in fact to be a kind of performance after all, and 'the class of exceptions thus swallows the supposedly normative class.'"⁶⁰ Briggs argues that both Austin and Searle allow the "descriptive" use of language to constitute a performative act. But this is a weakness in Austin's work and even in that of Searle. It separates the work of Briggs and Neufeld on "pure" speech acts from White and Botha on extended ones. At worst, the view tends "to reduce [speech acts] to a form of stylistics."⁶¹ This is what happens, we shall see, in Botha's work on John 4:1–42.

In chapter 4 of *Words in Action* Briggs begins with Searle's formulation "X counts as Y in context C," which creates an institutional fact, making possible illocutionary acts.⁶² This looks like the heart of Searle's approach, he says correctly. He contrasts this with the "neo-pragmatic" approach of Fish and Rorty, of whom he provides a useful critique.⁶³ He then expounds degrees of construal, helping to modify any undue polarization between fact-stating language and performative utterances. In the light of this he

---

57. Derrida, "Signature, Event, Context."
58. Briggs, *Words in Action*, 80–86.
59. Fish, "How to Do Things with Austin and Searle."
60. Briggs, "Speech-Act Theory"; Fish, *Is There a Text in this Class?* 231.
61. Briggs, *Words in Action*, 90.
62. Briggs, *Words in Action*, 105.
63. Briggs, *Words in Action*, 106–18.

Appendix

examines construal in biblical studies and argues for a hermeneutic of self-involvement.

This brings us to Brigg's Part Two, in which he examines specific interactions between biblical studies and speech-act theory. He rightly draws first on Donald Evans' *Logic of Self-Involvement*.[64] In the same vein, he examines the work of Neufeld.[65] This leads to his exploring New Testament language as confessing, forgiving, and teaching, all within a self-involving frame. (If only Rudolf Bultmann had explored the logic of self-involvement instead of existentialist philosophers, he might have maintained his many gains without incurring such disastrous losses.)

In his sixth chapter Briggs explores confessions of faith. Confessing Jesus Christ as Lord is a prominent theme. This brings a number of texts into play, such as 1 Cor 12:1-3. It also concerns such passages as Phil 2:5-11, 1 Cor 8:1-6, Col 1 and 1 Tim 3. Here he engages with Stephen Fowl (another of my former Ph.D. graduates) on the difference between form and function.[66] He especially interacts with Vernon Neufeld's book *The Earliest Christian Confessions* and Oscar Cullmann's book of the same title.[67] He also considers the relevant material in Dallas High, *Language, Persons and Belief*.[68] Briggs concludes, "Performing an utterance such as 'Jesus is Lord,' as it became a standard formula, counted as the act of committing oneself both to a certain standard (or content) of belief and also to certain future actions.... This self-involving dimension is precisely what is significant about confession."[69]

Briggs points out that studies of forgiveness have been few and far between. The two works he cites are from 1927 and 1946.[70]

---

64. Briggs, *Words in Action*, 148-66.

65. Briggs, *Words in Action*, 167-82.

66. Fowl, *The Story of Christ in the Ethics of Paul*, especially 31-32.

67. Neufeld, *The Earliest Christian Confessions*; and Cullmann, *The Earliest Christian Confessions*.

68. High, *Language, Persons, and Belief*, especially 164-84.

69. Briggs, *Words in Action*, 194.

70. Mackintosh, *The Christian Experience of Forgiveness*; and Taylor, *Forgiveness and Reconciliation*.

Developments in Speech-Act Theory and Biblical Studies

However, he comments, "To forgive is to perform a speech act."[71] He appeals to Gregory Jones and Joram Graf Haber for support.[72] Forgiveness is transformative, including attitudes and emotions. Emotions involve stances towards things, as Evans has argued. It affects far more than an isolated mental state. It may, for example, overcome resentment. The simple model of "I forgive you" illustrates this, especially if it is uttered by a priest or presbyter on behalf of God. It concerns more than introspection. Here, again, this involves institutional facts. Briggs comments, "In forgiving we may say that the forgiver . . . changes the institutional facts involved."[73] The significance of forgiveness arises from the transformed practices that derive from the act, not only from the act itself. Jones writes, "Forgiveness is the way in which God's love moves to reconciliation in the face of sin."[74] Briggs also draws on Miroslav Volf's *Exclusion and Embrace*.[75] Forgiveness, Briggs concludes, is "a strongly self-involving illocutionary act."[76]

Briggs finally explores teaching as a speech act. He appeals to Thomas Green for the notion that teaching performs logical acts, strategic acts, and institutional acts, matching respectively reasoning, organization, and direction of students.[77] Briggs stresses, "Illocutionary teaching acts might range from the evaluative judgement which dictates an enquiry . . . to the authoritative illocution which establishes and determines the issue at hand."[78] On the New Testament he allows a range of illocutionary acts from strong to weak. His "assertive" speech acts and "declarative" speech acts perhaps veer towards Austin's constatives.

Dieter Neufeld (1949–2015) was born in Paraguay but moved to Canada at the age of eight. He became Professor in the

---

71. Briggs, *Words in Action*, 219.
72. Jones, *Embodying Forgiveness*, 326; and Haber, *Forgiveness*, 29–57.
73. Briggs, *Words in Action*, 224.
74. Jones, *Embodying Forgiveness*, 5; cf. 59–64 and 83–91.
75. Volf, *Exclusion and Embrace*.
76. Briggs, *Words in Action*, 255.
77. Green, *The Activities of Teaching*, 4–9.
78. Briggs, *Words in Action*, 261.

Appendix

University of British Columbia, and President of the Canadian Society for Biblical Studies. I first met him at the Society for Biblical Literature and found an immediate kinship with common interests in speech-act theory. He draws usefully on Evans' notion of "self-involving" speech acts.[79] He applies this, not to prayer, but to confessions of belief in 1 John, together with the ethical commitments implied by these confessions. However, his insistence on "embodied communication" is also relevant to prayer.[80] We may consider his work more briefly than that of Briggs, since it simply concerns (for our purposes) only speech acts in 1 John.

Neufeld begins his work on speech acts in 1 John with the comment, "Language is a form of action and power. Discourse becomes responsible for creating reality and not merely reflecting it. The aim of the writer of 1 John is to bring about, not simply describe, the state of affairs his *kerygma* represents."[81] He adds, "The writer stands behind the words giving a pledge and personal backing that he or she is prepared to undertake commitments and responsibilities that are entailed in the extra-linguistic terms by the proposition which is asserted."[82] It is as if the writer gives his personal signature to what he says: "What is confessed implies certain commitments and becomes operative in acts of communion and in acts of love."[83]

After an introduction, the second chapter examines various approaches to 1 John and to the writer's opponents. He considers the work of Dodd, Bultmann, and Brown. In his third chapter he explores speech-act theory, in the context of varied uses of language. These are language-uses that have effects, and constitute a communicative event.[84] Predictably, like Austin, he uses the saying "I do" in a marriage ceremony as an example. He discusses illocutionary force. Because speech-act theory emphasizes

79. Neufeld, *Reconceiving Texts as Speech Acts*, 3.
80. Neufeld, *Reconceiving Texts as Speech Acts*, 41.
81. Neufeld, *Reconceiving Texts as Speech Acts*, vii–viii.
82. Neufeld, *Reconceiving Texts as Speech Acts*, viii.
83. Neufeld, *Reconceiving Texts as Speech Acts*, ix.
84. Neufeld, *Reconceiving Texts as Speech Acts*, 41.

extra-linguistic and social factors, Neufeld argues, speech acts became of special interest to Jacques Derrida in his desire to overturn the speaking/writing polarity.[85] Derrida argues that in the case of speech acts, "My communication must be repeatable—iterable—in the absolute absence of the receiver or any empirically determinable collectivity of receivers."[86] Neufeld does not follow Derrida in his more extreme speculations, but he approves the social context and the notion that often "the illocutionary force *constitutes* the self."[87] More specifically, he endorses Evans' notion that speech acts include a self-involving dimension, and his argument that much language relating to God is expressive or commissive.[88]

In his fourth chapter Neufeld emphasizes "testifying" as a major element in confessions of faith.[89] The readers are invited to share in "the perception, description, commitment and belief in what he has written."[90] These speech acts have effects upon the readers. But how different is this from the effect of corporate prayer? Neufeld regards "fellowship" in 1 John as "based on the reader's agreement with the author's views."[91] This involves a match or world-to-world fit. The writer's act of testifying "is based on the life made manifest but it also makes manifest the word of life to his readers/hearers."[92] All this is much more than "a passive recitation of orthodox Christological formulae."[93] The writer's writing is an act "which constitutes the self of the author and the readers."[94]

---

85. Neufeld, *Reconceiving Texts as Speech Acts*, 50; and Derrida, "Signature Event Context."

86. Derrida, "Signature Event Context," 179–80.

87. Neufeld, *Reconceiving Texts as Speech Acts*, 52 (my italics).

88. Neufeld, *Reconceiving Texts as Speech Acts*, 54.

89. Neufeld, *Reconceiving Texts as Speech Acts*, 74.

90. Neufeld, *Reconceiving Texts as Speech Acts*, 76.

91. Neufeld, *Reconceiving Texts as Speech Acts*, 78.

92. Neufeld, *Reconceiving Texts as Speech Acts*, 75.

93. Neufeld, *Reconceiving Texts as Speech Acts*, 79.

94. Neufeld, *Reconceiving Texts as Speech Acts*, 80.

Appendix

In his fifth chapter Neufeld discuses the slogans of his opponents. These are hypothetical speech-acts of boasting. He concludes, "The communicative end of 1 John is to invite the reader to join in a consideration of truths of the deepest import in which the recreative power of the word transforms the world view of the reader."[95] In chapters 6 and 7 he examines John's language about "the last hour and the Antichrist," and the confessions and denials of 1 John 4:1–4, 16, and 5:6. He concludes that 1 John constitutes a communicative event made up of a sequence of self-involving speech acts to which the author has committed himself.[96] This represents a much more dynamic and realistic portrait of 1 John, I argue, than we find in comparable works by Hugh White or Eugene Botha.

Hugh C. White of the Department of Religion in Rutgers University has edited the volume of the journal *Semeia* which is devoted to speech-act theory and biblical studies (41, 1988). In attempting to provide an overview of it he attempts to view literary speech-act theory in biblical studies in terms of three groups. One group mainly focusses on speech acts themselves; a "centre" group is broadly represented by Paul Grice on implicature of conversation; a third group mainly considers the social context of speech acts and "the constitution of subjectivity."[97] Alongside these three positions Mary Louise Pratt focusses on the social context of narrative.[98] White's interest is in the *literary* dimension of speech act theory, and he engages with relatively little which explicitly concerns biblical studies.

Many of White's comments concern writers of language or literature as such. For example he cites Wolfgang Iser as saying, "What is important to readers, critics, and authors alike is what literature *does,* and not what it *means*."[99] He next alludes to Austin,

---

95. Neufeld, *Reconceiving Texts as Speech Acts*, 95.
96. Neufeld, *Reconceiving Texts as Speech Acts*, 131.
97. White, "Speech Act Theory and Literary Criticism," 4.
98. Pratt, *Toward a Speech Act Theory of Literary Discourse*.
99. White, "Speech Act Theory," 2; and Iser, *The Narrative Act*, no page given.

Developments in Speech-Act Theory and Biblical Studies

with his distinction between descriptions and performatives, and his classic example of promise: "The utterance of the word itself, 'I promise' coincides with the act."[100] He adds that the concept of speech act is firmly connected with social context. He pursues his interest in literature by exploring the work of Richard Ohmann, before he turns to Grice and his four "maxims," to which we alluded above.[101] But, again, his use of Grice's co-operative principle is illustrated from English literature rather than biblical studies. Much of the remainder of White's essay concerns the subjectivity of the speaker or hearer, alluding especially to Derrida, Iser, Fish, and Paul de Man.

In a subsequent essay in *Semeia* White writes on "The Value of Speech Act Theory for Old Testament Hermeneutics."[102] He does discuss the promise/fulfilment schema of Zimmerli and Westermann, but much of his concern is with the new hermeneutic of Ernst Fuchs and Gerhard Ebeling. Elsewhere I have discussed the relation of this new hermeneutic to linguistic philosophy.[103] I am not convinced that Fuchs and Ebeling address the sophisticated complexities of British linguistic philosophy. Language-event (*Sprachereignis*) at best confuses illocutionary and perlocutionary acts, in spite of insights about linguistic methods. To this extent White is correct in asserting, "The new hermeneutic failed to carry biblical studies beyond historical exegesis because it was unable to develop an adequate means of applying its central understanding of the event character of language to ... biblical narratives."[104]

Eugene Botha's work on the Samaritan woman of John 4:1–42 concerns the woman's *conversation* with Jesus, and therefore he also carefully considers H. Paul Grice's published lectures *Logic*

---

100. White, "Speech Act Theory," 2.
101. White, "Speech Act Theory," 7-8.
102. White, "The Value of Speech Act Theory for Old Testament Hermeneutics."
103. Thiselton, "The Parables as Language Event"; and Thiselton, "The New Hermeneutic."
104. White, "Speech Act Theory," 58.

Appendix

and Conversation.[105] As Grice's title suggests, Grice works on refining the nature of conversation. He regards conversation not as a series or succession of different remarks, but as the production of "co-operative effects," which are guided in an "accepted direction."[106] He next points out that there will be certain gaps of what is left out in the conversation, to avoid overloading the flow of reciprocal information. These gaps, however, are in effect filled by conversational "implicature."[107]

Grice supports his argument by proposing four maxims that hold when any conversation takes place. First, he explains a maxim of *quantity*, i.e., the exchange of information should be economical, giving neither more nor less than is needed. Second, he formulates a maxim of *quality*, i.e., the communication should be truthful and sincere. Third, he produces a maxim of *relation*, i.e., information must be relevant. His fourth maxim concerns *manner*, i.e., it should be perspicacious. If all these are in place, a conversation can be reconstructed by implicature. (Grice gave some counterexamples, which did not fulfil all these maxims or expectations.) Botha insists that what Grice calls the co-operative principle is important for understanding biblical texts.[108] M. L. Pratt agrees with this.[109] Implicature is important, they both say, to understand exactly what the writer or speaker is implicating: "Speakers seldom supply full information or detail . . . and the sequence must be determined by implicature."[110]

Botha sees this implicature as equivalent to "background information," which is part of the narrative sequence. Bach and Hamish add to Grice's four maxims the maxim of *politeness*, which includes not revealing information that should not be revealed and not committing oneself to what the hearer does not want done.

    105. Botha, *Jesus and the Samaritan Woman*, 68–76; and Grice, *Logic and Conversation*.
    106. Grice, *Logic and Conversation*, 45.
    107. Grice, *Logic and Conversation*, 47.
    108. Botha, *Jesus and the Samaritan Woman*, 68.
    109. Pratt, *Towards a Speech Act Theory of Literary Discourse*.
    110. Botha, *Jesus and the Samaritan Woman*, 69.

Developments in Speech-Act Theory and Biblical Studies

They add a sixth maxim, the principle of *charity:* other things being equal, he says, we need to "construe the speaker's remarks so as to violate as few maxims as possible."[111] Linking this with Searle's "background," Bach and Hamish assert that this implied shared knowledge concerns "*mutual contextual beliefs.*"[112] They also describe this as a "linguistic presumption."[113] Often this is a presumption of literalness.[114] Finally, G. N. Leech adds two further maxims, which he calls "interpersonal rhetoric" and "textual rhetoric."[115] All this is valuable on conversation and "background," but how much light does it genuinely show on speech-act theory? Much of the author's efforts are devoted to Johannine style. The closest to speech-act theory probably concerns commitments.

Botha carefully considers shared knowledge, beliefs, and assumptions. Many speech acts, he says, do not have a literal illocutionary force.[116] On John 4, he declares, locutions, illocutions, and perlocutions all occur.[117] He comments, "Both readers and authors are aware that there are specific commitments which they have towards each other. It inevitably follows that this knowledge also shapes their way of communication."[118] From John 1–3, he continues, the mode of communication in John is mainly that of narrator, and it aims to give information about Jesus. But chapter 4 mainly depends on dialogue. First 4:7b–26 constitutes a first unit; with v. 27 giving a change in dialogue partners, this time with the disciples. Botha treats 4:31–38 as a new unit, and 4:39–42 as a final one. The effect of this, he argues, is to make readers participate in the dialogue, and also to leave room for implicature in supposed gaps in the narrative.[119]

111. Bach and Hamish, *Linguistic Communication and Speech Acts.*
112. Bach and Hamish, *Linguistic Communication and Speech Acts,* 5–6.
113. Bach and Hamish, *Linguistic Communication and Speech Acts,* 7.
114. Bach and Hamish, *Linguistic Communication and Speech Acts,* 61.
115. Leech, *Principles of Pragmatics,* 16.
116. Botha, *Jesus and the Samaritan Woman,* 72.
117. Botha, *Jesus and the Samaritan Woman,* 83.
118. Botha, *Jesus and the Samaritan Woman,* 89.
119. Botha, *Jesus and the Samaritan Woman,* 98.

Appendix

In the main dialogue the two speakers are "opposites": Jew and Samaritan; man and woman; rabbi and stranger. Speech-act theory make much of rules, conventions, and institutions. But this dialogue enters an unknown sphere.[120] If the woman were to accept the request of Jesus, she would be rejecting the commitments of her tradition. So she rejects the request. She reacts by posing a question and diverting the dialogue.[121] She appeals to Jacob, the highest authority she can think of on wells and springs, and addresses Jesus in the vocative, *kyrie* (lord or sir). The readers are given a "silence" in which to work out unstated facts about the woman. Botha declares, "The reader is immediately elevated to a level which the Samaritan woman cannot attain. . . . The author and readers are 'insiders,' but more than that they are in accord with the character of Jesus himself."[122]

Botha has shown a remarkable knowledge of Johannine scholarship and Johannine style, but how much have we advanced on speech-act theory? He clearly establishes that this is a dialogue in which the "maxims" of Grice, Pratt, and others may or may not apply. But this says more about Grice's conversational implicature than speech acts. Two problems are, first, that Botha follows Austin in regarding "constatives" as speech acts; and, second, that he does not draw a sharp and absolute line between illocutions and perlocutions. This becomes evident in his exposition of 4:27–31.[123] He concludes, "In speech act terms, the character of Jesus again employs a preventative in the form of a cognitive disclaimer when he contradicts (this) proverbial saying" [i.e., about Jews and Samaritans].[124] He is right, however, about the readers' involvement or what we might call with Evans "the self-involving" character of the narrative, and the inter-active relation of characters.[125] Botha contributes much on Johannine style, but is he

---

120. Botha, *Jesus and the Samaritan Woman*, 109–10.
121. Botha, *Jesus and the Samaritan Woman*, 118–19.
122. Botha, *Jesus and the Samaritan Woman*, 131.
123. Botha, *Jesus and the Samaritan Woman*, 165–68.
124. Botha, *Jesus and the Samaritan Woman*, 173.
125. Botha, *Jesus and the Samaritan Woman*, 190–97.

proportionately convincing on speech-act theory in John? At very least he underlines what has been said above about inter-personal relations, background, and implicature in Grice. Botha's work engages well with literary issues but does not show the same rigor as Briggs and Neufeld in the application of speech-act theory to biblical studies.

In 2006 I completed a short essay in my volume *Thiselton on Hermeneutics*. I repeated, "Speech-act theorists have identified promise as one of the clearest models of illocutionary action." I pointed out that "A hymn of praise may also enact or embody a promise in the context of worship [and] a sermon may embody acts of acclamation in the course of teaching or warning."[126] But this essay is too short to constitute a significant contribution to the subject.

In Conclusion

We have attempted to review further developments in speech act theory, especially in biblical studies. On the whole, these clarify and confirm our main contentions in this book, rather than explicitly advancing the discussion.

We considered the work of Evans on acknowledgements, onlooks, and self-involving speech acts. The notion of "onlooks" opened the way to explore further paths in theology (e.g., justification through faith). Recanati throws more light on performative force and also the crucial importance of context. So-called contextualism forbids over-easy generalization about speech acts as if they all assumed the same pattern.

Nicholas Wolterstorff demonstrates the clarity of thought which a distinguished philosopher brings to this subject. He uses everyday examples for what it means to "count as." He discusses institutions, such as the covenant, and "deputized discourse" in which God uses human agents to speak to humankind through the Bible. He affirms the best in Austin and Searle with exceptional

---

126. Thiselton, "More on Promising" 118; cf. 117–29.

sophistication. His work appears to affirm the main arguments of this book.

Richard Briggs provides one of the most comprehensive accounts of speech-act theory as it applies to biblical studies. The first half of *Words in Action* traces the recent developments in speech-act theory, while in the second half of the book he traces the speech acts of Christian confession, conveying forgiveness, and even teaching. His work is meticulous and convincing.

Dieter Neufeld applies speech-act theory specially to pronouncement in 1 John. He makes special use of "testimony" in this epistle. He brings the circumstances and message of the writer to life. It is difficult to see how the preoccupations with literary theory and style in Hugh White and Eugene Botha provide additional confirmation to the above arguments, except to display broader aspects of speech-act theory and biblical literary style. Nevertheless our discussion of developments beyond Austin and Searle show how the work of Wolterstorff, Briggs, and Neufeld, in particular confirm and enhance the arguments of this book.

Bibliography

Aquinas, Thomas. *Summa Theologiae*. ET and Latin. Oxford: Blackwell, 1963.
Ashwin, Angela. *The Book of a Thousand Prayers*. Grand Rapids: Zondervan, 2002.
Attridge, Harold W. *A Commentary on the Epistle to the Hebrews*. Philadelphia: Fortress, 1989.
Austin, John L. *How to Do Things with Words*. 1962. Reprint, Oxford: Clarendon, 1970.
Bach Kent, and Robert M. Harnish. *Linguistic Communication and Speech Acts*. Cambridge: MIT, 1979.
Barr, James. *The Semantics of Biblical Language*. Oxford: Oxford University Press, 1961.
Botha, J. Eugene. *Jesus and the Samaritan Woman: A Speech Act Reading of John 4:1-42*. Novum Testamentum Supplements, vol. 65. Leiden: Brill, 1991.
Briggs Richard S. *Reading the Bible Wisely*. London: SPCK, 2011.
———. "Speech-Act Theory." In *Dictionary for Theological Interpretation of the Bible*, edited by Kevin Vanhoozer et al., 763-66. Grand Rapids: Baker Academic, 2005.
———. *Words in Action: Speech-Act Theory and Biblical Interpretation*. Edinburgh: T. & T. Clark, 2001.
Brightman, Edgar S. *A Philosophy of Religion*. London: Skeffington, no date.
Brown, Alexandra R. *The Cross and Human Transformation: Paul's Apocalyptic Word in 1 Corinthians*. Minneapolis: Fortress, 1995.
Brümmer, Vincent. *What Are We Doing When We Pray?* Aldershot, UK: Ashgate, 2008.
Buber, Martin. *I and Thou*. ET. New York: Scribner, 1970.
Church of England Doctrine Commission. "God as Trinity: An Approach through Prayer." In *We Believe in God*, 104-21. London: Church House Publishing, 1987.
Clements Ronald E. *In Spirit and in Truth: Insights from Biblical Prayers*. Atlanta: John Knox, 1985.
Cullmann, Oscar. *The Earliest Christian Confessions*. London: Lutterworth, 1949.

Bibliography

Cupitt, Don. *Taking Leave of God*. London: SCM, 1981.
Danker, Frederick. *"epaggelia"* (promise). In *BDAG*, 355–56. Chicago: Chicago University Press, 2000.
Davis, Steven. "Anti-Individualism and Speech-Act Theory." In *Foundations of Speech-Act Theory*, edited by Savas L. Tsohatzidis, 208–19. London: Routledge, 1994.
Derrida, Jacques. *Limited Inc*. ET. Evanston, IL: Northwestern University Press, 1988.
———. "Signature, Event, Context." *Glyph* 1 (1977) 172–97.
Dürr, L. *Die Wertung des göttlichen Wortes im Alten Testament und im antiken Orient*. Leipzig: Hinrichs, 1938.
Eichrodt, Walther. *The Theology of the Old Testament*, Vol. 1. ET. London: SCM, 1961.
Evans, Donald D. *The Logic of Self-Involvement A Philosophical Study*. London: SCM, 1963.
Fann, K. T., ed. *Symposium on J. L. Austin*. London: Routledge, 1969.
Fish, Stanley. "How to Do Things with Austin and Searle: Speech-Act Theory and Literary Criticism." *Modern Language Notes* 9 (1976) 983–1025.
———. *Is There a Text in this Class?* Cambridge: Harvard University Press, 1980.
Fitzmyer, Joseph A. *The Gospel according to Luke 1–9*. Anchor Bible. New York: Doubleday 1981.
Fowl, Stephen. *The Story of Christ in the Ethics of Paul: An Analysis of the Function of the Hymnic Material in the Pauline Corpus*. JSNT, vol. 36. Sheffield, UK: JSOT, 1990.
Goldman, Alvin. *A Theory of Human Action*. Englewood Cliffs, NJ: Prentice Hall, 1970.
Gowan, Donald E. "Promise." In *The New Interpreter's Dictionary of the Bible*, Vol. 4, 617–19. Nashville: Abingdon, 2009.
Green, Joel B. *The Gospel of Luke*. NICNT. Grand Rapids: Eerdmans, 1997.
Green, Thomas F. *The Activities if Teaching*. New York: McGraw-Hill, 1971.
Greeven, Heinrich. *"euchomai"* and *"proseuchomai"* (to pray). In *TDNT*, Vol. 2, edited by G. Kittel and G. Friedrich, 775–808. 10 vols. Grand Rapids: Eerdmans, 1964–76.
Grether, O. *Name und Wort Gottes im Alten Testament*. BZAW. Giessen: Töpelmann, 1934.
Grice, H. Paul. "Logic and Conversation." In *Syntax and Semantics, vol. 3, Speech Acts*, edited by Peter Cole and Jerry L. Morgan, 41–58. New York: Academic Press, 1975.
Guthrie, George H. "Promise." In *Dictionary of the Later New Testament and Its Developments*, edited by R. P. Martin and Peter H. Davids, 967–70. Downers Grove, IL: IVP Academic, 1997.
Haber, Joram Graf. *Forgiveness*. Savage, MD: Rowman and Littlefield, 1991.
Haffemann, Ernest. "Promise." In *Dictionary of New Testament Theology*, vol. 3, edited by Colin Brown, 68–74. ET. Exeter, UK: Paternoster, 1978.

Bibliography

High, Dallas M. *Language, Persons, and Belief: Studies in Wittgenstein's Philosophical Investigations and Religious Uses of Language.* Oxford: Oxford University Press, 1967.

Hornsby, Jennifer. "Illocution and its Significance." In *Foundations of Speech-Act Theory*, edited by Savas L. Tsohatzidis, 187–207. London: Routledge, 1994.

Iser, Wolfgang. *The Narrative Act: Point of View in Prose Fiction.* Princeton: Princeton University, 1978.

Jacob, Edmund. *Theology of the Old Testament.* ET. London: Hodder & Stoughton, 1958.

Jeanrond, Werner G. *Text and Interpretation as Categories of Theological Thinking.* Dublin: Gil, 1988.

Jones, L. Gregory. *Embodying Forgiveness: A Theological Analysis.* Grand Rapids: Eerdmans, 1995.

Kant, Immanuel. *Religion within the Limits of Reason Alone.* ET. New York: Harper & Row, 1960.

Kierkegaard, Søren. *Fear and Trembling: Dialectical Lyric by Johannes de Silentio.* ET. London: Penguin, 1985.

Knight, G. A. F. *A Biblical Approach to the Doctrine of the Trinity.* Edinburgh: Oliver & Boyd, 1953.

———. *A Christian Theology of the Old Testament.* London: SCM, 1959.

Lane, William L. *Hebrews 1–8.* WBC. Dallas: Word, 1991.

Leech, G. N. *Principles of Pragmatics.* London: Longman, 1983.

Louw, Johannes P., and Eugene A. Nida, eds. *Greek-English Lexicon of the New Testament Based on Semantic Domains.* New York: UBS, 1989.

Lyons, John. *Introduction to Theoretical Linguistics.* Cambridge: Cambridge University Press, 1968.

Mackintosh, H. R. *The Christian Experience* of Forgiveness. London: Nisbet, 1927.

Marshall, I. Howard. *The Gospel of Luke.* NIGTC. Exeter, UK: Paternoster, 1978.

Miller, Patrick D. *They Cried to the Lord: The Form and Theology of Biblical Prayer.* Minneapolis: Fortress, 1994.

Moltmann, Jürgen. *Theology of Hope.* ET. London: SCM, 1967.

Morgan-Wynne, John. *Abraham in the New Testament.* Eugene, OR: Pickwick, 2020.

———. *Abraham in the Old Testament and Early Judaism.* Eugene, OR: Pickwick, 2020.

Neil, Charles, and J. M. Willoughby. *The Tutorial Prayer Book.* London: Church Book Room, 1959.

Neufeld, Dietmar. *Reconceiving Texts as Speech Acts: An Analysis of 1 John.* Leiden: Brill, 1994.

Neufeld, Vernon H. *The Earliest Christian Confessions.* Leiden: Brill, 1963.

Newman, Judith H. "Prayer." In *The New Interpreter's Dictionary of the Bible*, Vol. 2, edited by Katherine Doob Sakenfeld, 579–89. Nashville: Abingdon, 2006.

Bibliography

Noth, Martin. "The 'Re-presentation of the Old Testament in Proclamation." In *Essays on Old Testament Interpretation*, edited by Claus Westermann, 76–88. ET. London: SCM, 1963.

Pannenberg, Wolfhart. "Kerygma and History." In *Basic Questions in Theology*, vol. 1, 81–95. ET. London: SCM, 1970.

———. "Redemptive Event and History." In *Basic Questions in Theology*, vol. 1, 15–80. ET. London: SCM, 1970.

———. *Systematic Theology*, vol. 3. ET. Grand Rapids: Eerdmans, 1998.

Philo. *de sacrificiis Abelis et Caini*. In *The Works of Philo*, translated by C. D. Yonge, 94–111. Peabody, MA: Hendrickson, 1993.

———. *Legum allegoriae*. In *The Works of Philo*, translated by C. D. Yonge, 25–79. Peabody, MA: Hendrickson, 1993.

Pratt, Mary Louise. *Towards a Speech Act Theory of Literary Discourse*. Bloomington, IN: Indiana University Press, 1977.

Rad, Gerhard von. *Old Testament Theology*. ET. 2 vols. Edinburgh: SCM, 1965.

Recanati, François. *Meaning and Force: The Pragmatics of Performative Utterances*. Cambridge: Cambridge University Press, 1987.

———. *Perspectival Thought: A Plea for (Moderate) Relativism*. Oxford: Clarendon, 2007.

Sand, Alexander. "epaggelia, epaggellomai, epaggelma." In *Exegetical Dictionary of the New Testament*, Vol. 2, edited by Horst Balz and Gerhard Schneider, 13–16. ET. Grand Rapids: Eerdmans, 1991.

Schniewind, Julius, and Gerhard Friedrich. "*epaggellō*" (promise). In *TDNT*, vol. 2, edited by G. Kittel and G. Friedrich, 576–86. 10 vols. Grand Rapids: Eerdmans, 1964–76.

Searle, John R. *The Construction of Social Reality*. London: Penguin, 1995.

———. *Expression and Meaning: Studies in the Theory of Speech Acts*. Cambridge: Cambridge University Press, 1979.

———. *Speech Acts: An Essay in the Philosophy of Language*. Cambridge: Cambridge University Press, 1969.

Smith, C. Ryder. *The Bible Doctrine of Salvation*. London: Epworth, 1946.

Stiver, Dan R. "Ricoeur, Speech-Act Theory, and the Gospels as History." In *After Pentecost: Language and Biblical Interpretation, Scripture and Hermeneutics*, Vol. 2, edited by Craig Bartholomew, Colin Greene, and Karl Möller, 50–72. Carlisle, UK: Paternoster, 2001.

Taylor, Jeremy. *Rule and Exercises of Holy Living*. London: Royston, 1686.

Taylor, Vincent. *Forgiveness and Reconciliation: A New Testament Theology*. London: Macmillan, 1946.

Thiselton, Anthony C. "Hebrews." In *Eerdmans Commentary on the Bible*, edited by James D. G. Dunn and John W. Rogerson, 1451–82. Grand Rapids: Eerdmans, 2003.

———. "More on Promising." In *Thiselton on Hermeneutics: The Collected Woks and New Essays of Anthony Thiselton*, 117–29. Grand Rapids: Eerdmans, 2006.

Bibliography

———. "The New Hermeneutic." In *New Testament Interpretation*, edited by I. Howard Marshall, 308-33. Exeter, UK: Paternoster, 1977.

———. *New Horizons in Hermeneutics: The Theory and Practice of Transforming Reading.* London: Harper Collins, 1992.

———. "On the Logical Grammar of Justification in Paul." *Studia Evangelica* VII, edited by E. A. Livingstone, 491-95. Berlin: Berlin Academy, 1982.

———. "The Parables as Language Event: Some Comments on Fuchs's Hermeneutics in the Light of Linguistic Philosophy." *Scottish Journal of Theology* 23 (1970) 437-68.

———. "The Paradigm of Biblical Promise as Trustworthy, Temporal, Transformative Speech-Action." In Roger Lundin, Clarence Walhout, Anthony C. Thiselton, *The Promise of Hermeneutics*, 223-39. Grand Rapids: Eerdmans, 1999.

———. "The Supposed Power of Words in the Biblical Writings." *Journal of Theological Studies* 25 (1974) 283-99.

———. *The Two Horizons: New Testament Hermeneutics and Philosophical Description.* Exeter, UK: Paternoster, 1980.

Tsohatzidis, S. L., ed. *Foundations of Speech-Act Theory: Philosophical and Linguistic Perspectives.* London: Routledge, 1994.

Tyndale, William. *A Pathway into the Holy Scriptures.* In *Doctrinal Treatises*, 7-29. Cambridge: Cambridge University Press, 1848.

Ullmann, Stephen. *Principles of Semantics.* Oxford: Oxford University Press, 1957.

Urmson, J. O. "Austin's Philosophy." In *Symposium on J. L. Austin*, edited by K. T. Fann, 22-32. London: Routledge, 1969.

Vanderveken, Daniel. *Foundations of Illocutionary Logic.* Cambridge: Cambridge University Press, 1985.

Vanhoozer, Kevin J. "From Speech Acts to Scripture Acts: The Covenant of Discourse and the Discourse of the Covenant." In *After Pentecost: Language and Biblical Interpretation*, edited by Craig Bartholomew, Colin Greene, and Karl Möller, 1-49. SHS 2. Carlisle, UK: Paternoster, 2001.

———. *Is There a Meaning in this Text? The Bible, the Reader, and the Morality of Literary Knowledge.* Grand Rapids: Zondervan, 1998.

———. "The Semantics of Biblical Literature: Truth and Scripture's Diverse Literary Forms." In *Hermeneutics, Authority, and Canon*, edited by D. A. Carson and John Woodbridge, 53-104. Leicester, UK: IVP, 1986.

Volf, Miroslav. *Exclusion and Embrace: A Theological Exploration of Identity, Otherness, and Reconciliation.* Nashville: Abingdon, 1996.

Vriezen, Th.. C. *An Outline of Old Testament Theology.* ET. Oxford: Blackwell, 1962.

Warnock, Geoffrey J. "Some Types of Performative Utterance." In *Essays on J. L. Austin*, edited by Isaiah Berlin et al., 69-89. Oxford: Clarendon, 1973.

Watson, Duane F. "Rhetorical Criticism of Hebrews and the Catholic Epistles since 1978." *Currents in Research: Biblical Studies* 5 (1997) 175-207.

Weiser, Artur. *The Psalms: A Commentary.* ET. London: SCM, 1962.

Bibliography

Whitaker, Richard, and John R. Kohlenberger III. *The Analytical Concordance to the NRSV of the New Testament*. Oxford: Oxford University Press, 2000.

White, Hugh C. "Speech Act Theory and Literary Criticism." *Semeia* 41 (1988) 1–24.

———. "The Value of Speech Act Theory for Old Testament Hermeneutics." *Semeia* 41 (1988) 41–63.

Wittgenstein, Ludwig. *Philosophical Investigations*. English and German. Oxford: Blackwell, 1958.

———. *Zettel*. English and German. Oxford: Blackwell, 1967.

Wolterstorff, Nicholas. *Divine Discourse: Philosophical Reflections on the Claim that God Speaks*. Cambridge: Cambridge University Press, 1995.

———. "The Promise of Speech-Act Theory for Biblical Interpretation." In *After Pentecost: Language and Biblical Interpretation*, edited by Craig Bartholomew, Colin Greene, and Karl Möller, 73–90. SHS 2. Carlisle, UK: Paternoster, 2001.

Worley, D. R. "Fleeing Two Immutable Things: God's Oath-Taking." *Restoration Quarterly* 36 (1994) 222–36.

Ziesler, John A. *The Meaning of Righteousness in Paul: A Linguistic and Theological Enquiry*. Cambridge: Cambridge University Press, 1972.

Zimmerli, Walther. "Promise and Fulfilment." In *Essays on Old Testament Interpretation*, edited by Claus Westermann, 69–122. ET. London: SCM, 1963.

———. "Wort Gottes." In *Religion in Geschichte und Gegenwart*, Vol. 6, edited by Hans Dieter Betz, col. 1810. Tübingen: Mohr, 1962.

Index of Biblical References

Genesis

8:21—9:17	22
9:11	25, 28
9:26	49
11:31—12:5	22
12:2, 6, 8	22
13:15, 18	22
14:19	46, 49
15:5, 6, 17	33
15:18	22, 23
17:4	22
17:11–14, 17–19	23
18	5
21:16	69, 80
22	4, 23
24:12–14	70
27:28	57
27:33, 37	13, 58
28:1–4	57
32:9–12	70
47:29–30	37
49:2–27	50–51
50:7–13	36

Exodus

3:17	23
6:2–8	25
6:6	4
19:5–6	25
6:6	28
32:13	25, 28
32:30–35	5
32:31–32	71

Leviticus

26:40–41	26

Numbers

6:22–27	60, 72, 80
6:24–25	49
12:13	72
12:17	37
14:13–23	44
14:19	47
23:20	13
27:16–17	72
32:24	37

Deuteronomy

3:22	48
3:24	47
6:18	73
6:20–21	25
23:23	37
28:3	49
31:8	39
32:3	47
33:6–29	51
34:1–4	52

Index of Biblical References

Deuteronomy (cont.)

34:4	23
34:5–6	51

Joshua

1:3	24, 25
1:5, 9, 11	25
23:14	25

Judges

6:22	72
13:8–9	73
16:28	73

Ruth

1:8–9	57, 59
2:4, 12	60
2:10	49
3:10	60
4:14	60

1 Samuel

2:1	64
2:1–10	65

2 Samuel

5	4
5:6–10	25
7:9, 10, 13, 16	26
7:18–29	47, 57
17–25	25
22:31	21

1 Kings

3:16–28	73
4:20—10:29	26
8:23	48
17:17–24	73
18:36–37	74
19:20, 32	74

2 Kings

20:3	75

1 Chronicles

16:15–16	67
16:16, 17	24, 67
16:34	67

2 Chronicles

5:13	67
6:10	21
14:11	75
20:5–12	48

Psalms

12:6	21
21:1	40
69:31	65
77:7–9	26, 28
79:11	47
89:32–36	26
89:35–36	29
95:7–8	25, 35
98:1–3	63
100:3–5	68
103:17	65
117:2	63
118:1–4	63
119:50	21
119:148	21
121:8	39
150:2	47

Esther

4:7	37

Index of Biblical References

Isaiah

38:3	75
40:2, 10	27
42	33
43:2	38, 39
44:3	32
54:17	39
55:5–11	44
55:10–11	14
66:13	38

Jeremiah

23:29	14
29:11	39

Ezekiel

36:22, 23, 25	26
37:13, 14	26

Amos

3:1–2	26
7:1–6	5
7:7–9	5
8:1–3	5

Matthew

7:9	81
11:25	12
12:18–20	33
12:28	33
14:7	17
14:28–33	40
24	28
25:31	35

Mark

13	28
14:11	37

Luke

1:46–55	64–65
1:55	24
1:67–79	66
1:72	17, 24
5:17–26	33
24:49	32

John

3:16	39
4:1–42	93
4:27–31	102
11:25	12

Acts

1:4	32
2:28–39	32
3:25	24
7:17	24
16:32	32
13;34	17
23:6	35

Romans

4:3, 9	24, 33
4:3	33, 78
4:13	33, 78
4:13–16	34
4:20, 21	17
8:15–16	2, 6
8:26–27	2
9–11	34
9:4	34
9:31–32	34
10:3, 21	34
10:11	40
11:1	34
11:29	34
11:33–36	34

Index of Biblical References

1 Corinthians

1:18–25	72
1:18	15
2:1–5	15
8:1–6	93
12:1–3	93

2 Corinthians

1:20	31

Galatians

3:6	24
3:7	34, 78
3:13–14	33
3:16	17, 24
3:17	33
3:18	34
3:29	34

Philippians

2:5–11	93
4:7	38

Colossians

1:20–24	94

1 Thessalonians

4:13–17	27–18

Hebrews

4:1, 6	34, 78

6:13, 15, 16	17, 24
6:17–18	36
7:1–10	24
7:21	17
8:6	35
9:15–18	35
10:25	35
11:8–19	35
11:11	17
11:39	35

James

1:12	35
4:2	81

2 Peter

1:3–4	35
3:4, 9, 13	27

1 John

1:9	39
4:1–4	97
4:1–42	98
4:7–26	100
4:31–42	100
5:6	98

Revelation

15:3	63
22:20	27

Index of Names

Alston, William, 84, 86, 87
Anscombe, Elizabeth, 11, 89
Aquinas, Thomas, 5
Augustine, 68, 86
Austin, John L., 3, 4, 9, 10, 12, 13,
　　15, 19, 54, 57, 77, 78, 89, 91,
　　95, 99, 102, 104

Bach, Kent, and Harnish, Robert
　　M., 11, 100
Barr, James, 14
Barth, Karl, 4,
Botha, J. Eugene, 18, 19, 91, 92,
　　98, 99–102, 104
Briggs, Richard S., 12, 18, 19,
　　89–94, 95, 102, 103
Brightman, Edgar, 54
Brown, Alexandra, 15
Brown, Raymond, 95
Brümmer, Vincent, 5, 43, 54, 57,
　　78
Buber, Martin, 1, 77
Bultmann, Rudolf, 4, 32, 93, 95

Calvin, John, 3,
Cerf, Walter, 19
Church of England Doctrine
　　Commission, 2
Clements, Ronald, 45, 46, 47, 50,
　　63–64, 66–67
Cullmann, Oscar, 93
Cupitt, Don, 5, 44

Davis, Stephen, 3, 54
Derrida, Jacques, 91, 92, 96, 97, 99
Dodd, Charles H., 95
Dürr, L., 13, 14

Ebeling, Gerhard, 4, 98
Eichrodt, Walter, 10,
Evans, Donald, 3, 4, 9, 11, 56–57,
　　62, 68, 78, 82–83, 89,, 93, 94,,
　　95, 97, 101, 102

Fann, K. T., 18
Fish, Stanley, 92
Fitzmyer, Joseph, 65
Fowl, Stephen, 93
Frei, Hans, 89
Fuchs, Ernst, 98

Goldman Alvin, 86
Green, Joel B., 65
Green, Thomas, 94
Grether, O., 13
Grice, H. P., 84, 88, 90, 91, 97, 98,
　　99, 101, 102
Green, Thomas, 95
Guthrie, George, 31

Haber, Joram Graf, 94
Hampshire, Stuart, 18
Hornsby, Jennifer, 90
High, Dallas M., 93

Index of Names

Iser, Wolfgang, 97, 99

Jacob, Edmund, 13, 14,
Jeanrond, Werner, 91
Jones, Gregory, 94

Kant, Immanuel, 5, 43-44, 54, 69, 79, 87
Kierkegaard, Søren, 4, 23
Knight, G. A. F., 14
Kohlenberger, John R.

Leech, G. N., 100
Luther, Martin, 1, 77

Man, Paul de, 99
Marshall, I. Howard, 65
Miller, Patrick D., 47, 56-57, 60, 62-63, 67-68, 70, 71, 78
Moltmann, Jürgen, 12, 77
More, Thomas, 44

Neil, Charles, and Willoughby, J. M., 68
Neufeld, Dieter, 12, 18, 19, 21, 91, 92, 94-98, 102, 103
Neufeld, Vernon, 94
Nolland, John, 65
Noth, Martin, 25

Ohmann, Richard, 98

Pannenberg, Wolfhart, 1, 12, 29, 77
Pedersen, J., 14
Plantinga, Alvin, 85
Pratt, Mary Louise, 97, 99, 101

Rad, Gerhard von, 12, 13, 21

Recanati, François, 3, 4, 9, 11, 84, 91, 102
Ricoeur, Paul, 9, 89
Rorty, Richard, 92

Schleiermacher, Friedrich, 88
Searle, John R., 3, 4, 9, 10, 11, 17, 18, 56-57, 78, 86, 89, 91, 92, 100, 104
Smith, C. Ryder, 71
Stiver, Dan, 88, 89
Strawson, P. F., 18

Thiselton, Anthony C., 85 n.14, 102
Tsohatzidis, S. L., 11,
Tyndale, William, 3, 77

Urmson, J. O., 18, 19,

Vanderveken, Daniel, 11
Vanhoozer, Kevin, 88
Volf, Miroslav, 95
Vriezen, Th. C., 5

Warnock, Geoffrey, 18, 53, 56, 61
Watson, Duane, 91
Weiser, Artur, 28-29
Westermann, 99
White, Hugh c., 18, 91, 92, 97-99, 104
Wittgenstein, Ludwig, 15, 56, 84, 92
Wolterstorff, Nicholas, 12, 85-89, 91, 102, 103
Worley, D. R.,

Ziesler, John, 84
Zimmerli, W., 13, 29-30, 31, 99

Index of Subjects

Aaronic blessing, 60
Abba! Father, 2
Abraham as paradigms case, 22
Abraham, Isaac, and Jacob, 7
absence of institutional mechanism,
acknowledgement, 62, 82
adoration and praise, 43
ambassador or secretary, examples of, 86
ambiguity, 18
apologize, approve, 53
appoint or authorize, 77
archangel's call, 28
authorial discourse and performance interpretation, 88

Balaam and Balak, 37
baptism and the Lord's Supper, 3,
Behabitives, 53–54, 56, 59, 80
blessing of Melchizedek, 49
blessing of Moses, 51
blessing, 49–50, 62–68
Brightman on "best possible," 54
brute facts, 3, 10

Canaanite had social organisation, 23, 50
causal force, 4, 71
change of mind on God's part? 71
change of circumstances, 43
change or describe? 11

changes of situation, 3, 9, 56
changing situations in the world, 3, 11, 66
charity, 100
Church of England Doctrine Report, 2
Church, law, property, 10
churchly faith (Kirchenglaube) in Kant, 43
commissive performative utterances, 12, 53
commitments and responsibilities, 9, 13, 77, 82, 85
complaint, motivation, petition, response, 71
conditions for answered prayer, 54
confession and contrition, 46, 92
confessions, early Christian, 18, 92
constatives, 18
constitutive rules, 89
context, 83
contextually limited promises, 40
contingency, 29
contrition or confession, 80
conventions, 86, 101
cooperative effects, 99
count generation, 85
covenant as an institutional fact, 81
covenant promises, 10, 72
covenant signs, 23

115

Index of Subjects

covenant with Abraham, 22,
covenant with Noah, 22
covenant, 2, 6, 10, 11, 13, 28, 83, 87

Daily Manna Promise Box, 38
David's praise and blessing, 47, 57
Death of Moses, 51
declaration of blessing, 57, 59
declaration of marriage as analogy, 58
declarative speech act, 93
difference of fit: words and reality, 11, 59
directives in Searle, 17–18,
direction of fit, 80
divine dialogue, 6, 77
divine guidance, 70
diverse functions, 15
double agency discourse, 85, 87
duck-rabbit, 83
dynamic and static thought, 15

eight-century prophets, 26
Elijah and prophets of Baal, 73–74
Eli's sons, 64
Eliezer's prayer, 70, 79
Entreaty as act, 54
epistemology, 83
eschatological dimension of promise, 12
eschatology, 83
evaluation, 63
expositives, 53–54
extra-textual historical milieu, 21
Ezekiel, 2

Forgiveness, 92
fulfilment, 31

generalisations about words, 14
generalizing promises, 39
Gentiles, mission to, 34
Galilee and Gentiles, 65
God:

God as changing things, 63
God as Father, 2
God as incomparable and unchanging, 5
God's limitation of choice in covenant, 2, 83
grace, 83
guarantee or pledge, 16,

Hannah's and Mary's prayer of praise, 62–64
happy functioning of performatives, 4,
healing miracles and peace, 33
Hebrew concordances and lexica, 16
Hermeneutical circle, 88
Hezekiah's prayer, 74–75
History and fiction, 89
Holy Spirit as prompter of prayer, 77–78
Holy Spirit, 32–33,
Human shortcomings, 28
Hymns of praise, 63

Illocutions and conventions, 84–87
illocutions, 4, 57, 66, 84, 95
illocutions, illocutionary force, 72, 86
implicature, 97–98, 101
implicit performatives, 16
implicit promises, 12
indiscriminate appropriation, 38
individualism or solipsism, 3, 13
institutions and conventions, 15, 83
institutional backing, 5
institutional facts, 3, 10, 17, 77, 86, 89
institutional force, 4, 86
institutional mechanism absent, 13
iterability, 92
intercession of Moses, 71

Index of Subjects

intercessory prayer, 5, 43, 45,
interpersonal relationship, 5, 76, 99
irrevocable validity of gift, 30
Isaac's blessing, 57
I-Thou, 1–2, 77

Jesus Christ, 11, 24, 31
Judges, period of, 72–73
Justification by grace through faith, 83

lament or complaint, 48, 80

makes glad, makes an heir, 3,
Mary in the Magnificat, 64
Maxims, 98
Miriam's leprosy, 71
Moses as a mediator, torn in two, 71
mourning, act of, 56
multiple illocutionary act, 90
mutual contextual beliefs, 100

Naomi's blessing, 57, 59
notion of the best possible, 54

oath as formalizing commitment, 17
once-for-all, 31
onlooks, 83

pardon, 46
parousia or final coming, 27
patience as waiting for the future, 12,
performative and declarative speech, 58
performative utterances in Austin, 15, 77
perspectival thought, 83
Peter's speech, 24
petitionary prayer, 45, 80
pledge or personal backing, 9

pledge and binding commitment, 24, 94
politeness, 99
potential illocutions, 83
power-laden words, 13, 14,
prayer:
    prayer as Divine dialogue, 1–2
    prayer as interpersonal, 44
    prayer initiated by God, not humans, 1–3
    prayer as interpersonal, 1–6
    prayer as praise, 47
    prayer of Moses, 45
    prayer or magic, 58
    prayer, as speech act, 53–55, 62–65
    prayer, performative act of, 80
    prayer: different types of, 43–52, 80
promise:
    promise as a term, 77, 102
    promise as contradicting the present, 12
    promise, frequency of, 32
    promise of God, 1–6, 77
    promise to Abraham, 78
    promise, 1–6, 77–79
    promises as commitments, 9–10,
    promise as paradigm, 10, 77
    promises as reliable, 36
    promises as tying our hands, 77–78
    promises as speech-acts, 12, 85
    promise boxes, 38–39
    promises limited by context and time, 38
    promise vs. statement, 19
propositional content, 85
purely rational prayer, 5

rational faith (*Vernunftglaube*) in Kant 4
reader-response theory, 92
request to God to act, 75

Index of Subjects

rhetoric, 4
rhetorical persuasion or elocutions? 15, 72
rights and duties, 87, 90
royal decree, analogy of, 4
rules of chess, 86

seeing as, 83
self-involvement, 69, 78, 90, 95
shopping list analogy, 11
social context, 98
Sodom and Gomorrah, 23
Solomon's praise, 48
Solomon's prayer, 73
Speech acts:
   speech acts, 9–20, 21, 77
   speech act as unstoppable, 27
   speech act of commitment, 20
   speech-act theory, 3–6, 83, 86–87, 91
spoken reason, 6
status and role, 11
Stephen's speech, 24
subjective view of prayer, 44, 79
supplication and entreaty, 48

taste, different meanings of, 14

temporary setbacks, 29
thanking or praising, 53, 66
therapeutic meditation, 5, 44, 54, 58
Two Horizons, 83
today of fulfilment, 31, 35
traditional view of prayer, 69
transformation, 12, 93
trust and security, 10,
two evaluations, 83

umpire's "Out," 89
unconditional promises, 37
union of wills with God, 54
universal appropriation of promise, 38–39, 79

verdictive performative act, 63
vitality of promise, 29

wholly Other, 28
word and thing, 14
words and actions, 44

Zechariah, Elizabeth, and Mary's blessings, 65, 67

www.ingramcontent.com/pod-product-compliance
Lightning Source LLC
Chambersburg PA
CBHW032232080426
42735CB00008B/821